"Romero and Liou com[bine] with decades of pastoral [...] [...] under-stand the intersection of biblical ideas and the tools offered by critical race theory. This deeply nuanced Christian reflection is desperately needed for the divisive time in which we find ourselves."

—**Sandra María Van Opstal**, pastor, activist, author, and founder of Chasing Justice

"This book should be required reading for anyone seeking to explore the intersection of critical race theory and Christian Scripture. With the erudition of scholars and the care of pastors, Romero and Liou helpfully demystify the basic tenets of CRT, critique popular misconceptions, and highlight various points of resonance (and dissonance) with biblical truth. Firmly anchored in singularly Christian eschatological hope, *Christianity and Critical Race Theory* adds much-needed light to a public conversation that tends to be defined by the dimness of ignorance and the heat of reactionary culture-war passions."

—**Duke Kwon**, coauthor of *Reparations: A Christian Call for Repentance and Repair*

"In *Christianity and Critical Race Theory*, Romero and Liou provide the first comprehensive, insightful, and timely story of the connection between Christian theology, Scripture, and critical race theory. This book is a significant contribution to the fields of critical race theory and liberation theology. Critical race scholars today and in the future will be served by this gift."

—**Daniel G. Solórzano**, University of California-Los Angeles

"Many Christians say, 'All truth is God's truth.' Robert Chao Romero and Jeff Liou heartily agree and invite us to consider how critical race theory contains important truths that help us understand the complexities of racism in our society. No mere apologetic, this book models how to have both deep appreciation and thoughtful critique while also seeking deep faithfulness to God and a faithful witness to the fullness of the gospel in our world. Instead of letting the winds of hype sway us one way or another, we should walk forward with clarity, courage, and hope."

—**Vincent Bacote**, Wheaton College

"When tricky questions come up about critical race theory, Romero and Liou are the first people that I turn to. Their deep commitment to theological reflection and their nuanced understanding about race make them reliable, insightful, and helpful guides. Sidestepping the cultural mines that make conversations around race tricky, Romero and Liou help readers understand the larger dynamics, orient them in Christian ways, provide helpful insights, and bring clarity to complicated topics. Thank you for this resource!"

—**Nikki Toyama-Szeto**, executive director, Christians for Social Action

# Christianity and Critical Race Theory

## A Faithful and Constructive Conversation

Robert Chao Romero
and Jeff M. Liou

Baker Academic
*a division of Baker Publishing Group*
Grand Rapids, Michigan

Published by Baker Academic
a division of Baker Publishing Group
www.bakeracademic.com

Printed in the United States of America

Library of Congress Cataloging-in-Publication Data
Names: Romero, Robert Chao, 1972– author. | Liou, Jeff M., 1979– author.
Title: Christianity and critical race theory : a faithful and constructive conversation / Robert Chao Romero, and Jeff M. Liou.
Description: Grand Rapids, Michigan : Baker Academic, a division of Baker Publishing Group, [2023] | Includes bibliographical references and index.
Identifiers: LCCN 2022033379 | ISBN 9781540965196 (paperback) | ISBN 9781540966148 (casebound) | ISBN 9781493438327 (ebook) | ISBN 9781493438334 (pdf)
Subjects: LCSH: Critical race theory—Religious aspects—Christiantiy. | Race relations—Religious aspects—Christianity. | Discrimination—Religious aspects—Christianity. | Christian sociology. | United States—Race relations.
Classification: LCC BT734.2 .R66 2023 | DDC 230.089—dc23/eng/20221004
LC record available at https://lccn.loc.gov/2022033379

Some names and details of the people and situations described in this book have been changed or presented in composite form in order to ensure the privacy of those with whom the authors have worked.

Baker Publishing Group publications use paper produced from sustainable forestry practices and post-consumer waste whenever possible.

23   24   25   26   27   28        7   6   5   4   3   2   1

To family and friends adrift, longing for welcome,
and to those working to make room.
—Jeff Liou

To my sisters and brothers who are taking the hard
hits so that the church might "become mature,
attaining to the whole measure of the fullness of
Christ" (Eph. 4:13). We see you. We thank you.
—Robert Chao Romero

# Contents

# Acknowledgments

Our spouses became friends before we became coauthors. After that, I (Jeff) would quickly come to realize the asset that I had in knowing the Romeros. I was a teaching assistant for a class that Robert took for his ongoing learning, and then I asked him to guide me in a directed reading during my doctoral program. Our friendship with the Romeros has been warm and fruitful. We are grateful.

I am also grateful to the many colleagues in InterVarsity Christian Fellowship who have helped to sharpen the way I talk about and teach theology. In so many ways, this writing project is yet another experiment in formulating theological ways of engaging the academy within which our staff operate. I am grateful to the senior leaders who have asked me to brief them on critical race theory (CRT); to Jason Jensen for his support of my scholarly vocation; to the Spiritual Foundations team, who listens so carefully to help me hear God's great love for our staff; to Greg Jao for opportunities to represent us externally; and to many other colleagues, like Silvia Kim Ahn, for engaging me with honesty and curiosity.

I have had the great pleasure of speaking about CRT alongside encouraging Christian scholars and ministers. I owe thanks to Nathan Cartagena, Korie Little Edwards, and Soong-Chan Rah for modeling scholarly hunger and thirst for righteousness, all for Jesus's sake. The opportunity to clarify my thinking through writing came when Matthew Kaemingk asked me to contribute a chapter from our shared theological tradition. Of course, I continue to learn from the way that Richard Mouw engages contentious cultural moments and "beholds" his interlocutors.

I do not take for granted those in our church who were deeply formed by intentional color blindness yet chose to extend me credit and strained to understand why this conversation is so important for the church. Those who have been willing to betray outmoded ministry models and comfortable theology in order to become beloved community have begun well.

Lastly, my wife and children have observed my ups and downs researching and writing in the margins of my work time, homelife, attentional capacity, and physical energy. As much as this writing is an exercise in integration, so I hope and pray our life together is integrated by the One in whom all things consist. I learn more and more from each of you every day. Thanks be to God!

---

I (Robert) wish to thank my CRT colleagues, especially in the fields of education and law, for producing scholarship that has given me and so many others the language to understand and process our own racialized experiences in the United States. Many thanks also to Nathan Cartagena of Wheaton College, who has been a pioneer of the intersection of Christianity and CRT and a dear compañero on the journey. We're thankful for your important book on the same topic.

Gratitude is owed to Bob Hosack for the invitation to write this book back at the 2019 meeting of the American Academy of Religion. Little did we know what was to come and how the world would change. I also wish to thank my mother, Dr. Ruth Chao Romero, for reading and commenting on drafts of my writing. I'm so blessed by her love and support and to have a powerful mother with a PhD in English. Finally, the biggest appreciation is owed to my wife, Erica. The ideas of this book have been jointly forged over the past seventeen years of life and ministry together.

# Introduction

## Critical Race Theory in Christianity

I (Robert) am an "Asian-Latino." My father immigrated to Texas from Chihuahua, Mexico, as a young child in the 1950s, served in Vietnam, and worked as a K–12 and higher education administrator for many years. My mother came to Los Angeles in the 1950s, but she came as a religious refugee. My maternal grandparents, Calvin and Faith Chao, founded InterVarsity Christian Fellowship in China in the 1940s but were forced to flee with their eight children to the United States because my grandfather was on a communist hit list. My parents met and married while part of my Chinese grandparents' ministry to young adults, and I was born not too long afterward in East Los Angeles. Though I am not *that* old, I entered elementary school just a few years after the public schools of Los Angeles were desegregated by judicial decree in 1970.

When I was growing up, race was very much a live issue. The town where we lived was in the San Gabriel Valley and was mostly white. "Whiteness" was the standard to which all aspired for acceptance. At one point, my childhood home was ransacked and our car flooded with water, presumably by someone who did not like our multicultural family moving into the neighborhood. Because I present as phenotypically Latino, I was sometimes called "beaner." I denied my Chinese heritage for many years after experiencing a traumatic racial microaggression during my early elementary years. Ironically, my Mexican ancestry—and the Romero family's "Spanish" identity—granted me the closest proximity to whiteness, so I fully embraced that singular racial identity throughout my childhood. Nonetheless, I experienced plenty of discrimination based on my Latino identity as well. I was excluded from gifted and talented education (GATE) despite my sincere pleadings, and I was once accused of plagiarism by a teacher who was surprised by the quality of my academic work. I distinctly remember an incident in high school when I was trying to impress a white female classmate by sharing my dream of becoming a lawyer and was callously told, "I'd never hire a Mexican lawyer." I can also tell the usual stories of being racially profiled by police and tracked into shop classes that involved less academic rigor and that historically channeled Latinos[1] into the work-

1. The terms *Latino, Latina, Latinx, Hispanic, Chicano, Chicana,* and *Chicanx* are contested labels that reflect the diverse social identities of those of Latin American descent living in the United States. The term *Latino* refers specifically to a man of Latin American descent and sometimes is used to refer to both men and women in a general sense. The term *Latina* refers specifically to a woman of Latin American descent. In order to counter the patriarchal influences within the Latino community, I and others sometimes choose to deliberately use both terms (*Latina/o*) when speaking of the larger community. *Latinx* is a newer term that is utilized mostly by academics and members of the younger generation both to challenge chauvinistic bias and to emphasize a belief in gender fluidity beyond the traditional male-female binary. The term *Hispanic* holds the same general meaning as *Latino* but is controversial among academics and activists because it tends to emphasize the Spanish cultural roots of Latin American countries to

ing class, as well as many other common experiences faced by students of color.

After eventually graduating from law school and completing my PhD in history, I became a professor of Chicana/o studies at UCLA in 2005. I began to teach legal-studies courses such as Latinas/os and the Law: Comparative and Historical Perspectives; the History and Politics of Affirmative Action; Chicano Public Interest Law; and Chicano Legal History. As reflected in their various titles, these courses explore the wide-ranging experiences of Latinas and Latinos within the American legal system over the past two centuries. They examine landmark appellate decisions and litigation efforts in a wide variety of areas, such as immigration, voting rights, employment, jury service, language discrimination, bilingual education, criminal law, and educational admissions. These courses also critically assess the role of legal principles and litigation in improving the position of Latinas and Latinos in American society. Though I did not plan it, over the years I have found my own racialized experiences, and those of my students, reflected in my courses. Xenophobia: check. Language discrimination: check. Employment discrimination: check. Educational segregation: double check. Racial profiling by police: triple check.

It is the stories of my students, both at UCLA and at extramural campus ministry, that have impacted me the most. I'll never forget Angelica. Angelica grew up in an immigrant

---

the exclusion of indigenous cultural influences. The term *Chicano* is an ethnic-political social identity term that emerged in the civil rights era of the 1960s to refer to a person of Mexican American cultural origins who embraces both European and indigenous ancestry and who is dedicated to social activism on behalf of the Mexican American community. The academic discipline of Chicana/o studies emerged from the historic Chicano civil rights movement. In this book, I have chosen to refer to the broader community of people of Latin American descent as *Latino*, but sometimes I use both *Latino* and *Latina* when seeking to emphasize gender inclusivity.

3

family. She was a strong student who earned admission to a good local university. After beginning her college studies, however, she quickly became battered by experiences of injustice. One day Angelica's mom was rushed to the local hospital. The doctors examined her and determined that she needed emergency surgery. A week later, she returned to the hospital because of continued pain. As it turns out, the hospital had made a mistake in her procedure.

Later, Angelica's mom went back to the hospital yet again because she noticed some strange and disturbing physical symptoms. As part of the previous surgery, she had been given a blood transfusion, but the blood had been infected with a disease. When confronted, the hospital denied all wrongdoing. Because Angelica's mom did not have many economic resources, she was unable to hire an attorney, and no one would take her case. But the story gets even worse. Several years later, during the process of applying for her green card, Angelica's mom suffered the further indignity of having to write what amounted to a note of apology to the US government for having acquired the insidious disease. Eventually, Angelica dropped out of college under the weight of these life challenges and collective stressors.

John's story has also never left me. John was a first-generation college student. He grew up in an immigrant church and loved theology. John was an undocumented student who had beaten all the odds by getting accepted into an Ivy League school as a freshman. A caring high school teacher helped sponsor John for his first year of study, but like Angelica, John became distracted by racist structural and systemic forces that were beyond his control and struggled to maintain his academic focus. In one conversation, John shared about family members who had been wrongly deported after reporting a crime to the local police. In a separate incident, John's father was also later deported. As a responsible son, John chose to surrender his scholarship money so that his mother and siblings might have enough for food and rent. His teenage sister was subsequently arrested by ICE and recklessly deported late one evening onto the streets of a Mexican border town. As a vulnerable freshman, John tried to find spiritual and emotional support in a well-known campus ministry but was called a "criminal."

As a lawyer, historian, and pastor, I know that the racialized experiences of John and Angelica are not isolated and that they are, in fact, part of larger structures and systems that have been supported by centuries of law, policy, and even theology. The historical realities of such laws and policies—as well as their pernicious effects—have been well documented and rigorously analyzed by multidisciplinary scholars in the social sciences, humanities, and STEM fields for decades. Critical race theory (CRT)—the focus of this book—is just one of many academic lenses that have examined the ways in which race, ethnicity, and culture have operated to shape US laws, policies, and institutions over the past four hundred years.

I first came to use CRT as an academic tool about a decade ago. Around that time, I was helping to lead a tour of urban Latina/o students at the university I worked at, together with a Christian urban youth organization. After meeting the students, I walked with them to the elevator doors of a building on campus. Around twenty Latina/o high school students were with me, and when we arrived at the elevator, I pressed the elevator button a few times, like I normally do. In response, another worker from the university told me I didn't have to press the button so many times; it would work if I pressed it just once.

About half the students walked with me onto the elevator. We pressed the button for our floor, and the staff member pressed the button for his floor. We noticed that, for some reason, the buttons for several other floors were also lit up (think of the famous scene from *Elf*). Had one of the teenagers pressed them? Or were they lit up for some other reason? The staff member made some seemingly angry and disrespectful comments, appearing to blame the students. (As it turns out, the students had not pressed the buttons.) I was very mad, and I told the worker, "These students are here at college for the first time."

The staff member then looked at the students and said that they would need to buck up if they wanted to come to college.

I was infuriated. As I expressed my displeasure, he got off on his floor without saying a word. I then apologized to the students for what they had just experienced. But then, with tears in their eyes, they told me, "It's OK; we're used to it." I was deeply touched by the homemade, handwritten cards I later received, which said, "Thank you for speaking up for us."

As God would have it, around that same time I was teaching my first graduate class on Chicana/o legal history and CRT. CRT gave me the language to describe what I experienced that day, for not the first or the last time: a microaggression. Microaggressions are small acts of racism that those of us who are BIPOC (black, indigenous, and people of color) experience on a regular basis in the United States. Often they take the form of rude or arrogant racially tinged comments or actions. Each individual microaggression is painful in itself, but collectively they can take an especially heavy emotional toll. In their book *Critical Race Theory: An Introduction*, Richard Delgado and Jean Stefancic write that microaggressions, "like water dripping on sandstone, . . . can be thought of as small acts of racism, consciously or unconsciously perpetrated, welling up from the assumptions about racial matters most of us absorb from the cultural heritage in which we come of age in the United States. These assumptions, in turn, continue to inform our public civic institutions—government, schools, churches—and our private, personal, and corporate lives."[2]

As a professor, lawyer, historian, and pastor, I've continued to teach and write professionally about CRT ever since teaching that class. As mentioned above, CRT has given me the language to describe my own racialized experiences and those of many people I know. Over the years, I've come to one basic conclusion: CRT is *helpful*. I have found it to be helpful as a bridge for Christian witness, theological reflection, and pastoral ministry. Before I explain why, let me first explain more about the origins of CRT and what it is.

*What is CRT?* Critical race theory examines the intersection of race, racism, and US law and policy. In other words, it looks at how US laws and public policy have been manipulated and constructed over the years to preserve privilege for those considered "white" at the expense of those who are people of color. For example, how did racism infect US law and policy through slavery and Jim Crow segregation, and how does racism continue to cripple our legal, educational, political, corporate, and public health institutions? According to Delgado and Stefancic,

> The critical race theory movement is a collection of activists and scholars interested in studying and transforming the relationship among race, racism, and power. The movement

2. Delgado and Stefancic, *Critical Race Theory*, 2.

considers many of the same issues that conventional civil rights and ethnic studies discourses take up, but places them in a broader perspective that includes economics, history, context, group- and self-interest, and even feelings and the unconscious. Unlike traditional civil rights, which stresses incrementalism and step-by-step progress, critical race theory questions the very foundations of the liberal order, including equality theory, legal reasoning, Enlightenment rationalism, and neutral principles of constitutional law.[3]

Critical race theory began as a movement among legal scholars in the 1970s and 1980s because most American law schools ignored the topic of race and racism altogether. In my own law school experience at Berkeley, I found this to be true. CRT, whose intellectual father figure is the late Derrick Bell, has continued to build as an intellectual movement, and it has spawned offshoots such as LatCrit (Latino critical race theory) and an Asian American CRT movement. LatCrit folks like myself research and advocate topics such as immigration, education, and voting rights. CRT has also been adopted and developed by scholars of other disciplines, including education and history.

CRT offers four decades worth of empirical, interdisciplinary observations of how culture, ethnicity, and race have operated in US history. Just as a Christian scientist might say that all truth is God's truth and that, therefore, the scientific truths found in test tubes and laboratory experiments may be considered part of God's general revelation, so a proponent of CRT might offer empirical truths about how race has operated as a legal and social category throughout the past four hundred years of US history. That being said, CRT represents a diverse body of theory and reflection, and I do

3. Delgado and Stefancic, *Critical Race Theory*, 3.

not agree with it all. For that matter, not all CRT theorists and practitioners agree with one another. As an example of a valid critique of CRT, my coauthor, Jeff Liou, points out that CRT largely lacks a hopeful eschatological vision of the beloved community of all. I agree, and I believe, along with Jeff, that the addition of such an overarching theological vision could be a significant Christian contribution to CRT. Another legitimate criticism is that some CRT analysis can skew Marxist, though certainly not all or even most of it.[4] As a member of a Christian family who was forced to flee China because my pastor grandfather was threatened with death for his religious leadership and convictions, I am certainly not a Marxist. But prophetic criticism of economic and racial injustice does not mean that one is a Marxist—just look at the more than two thousand verses of Scripture that speak of God's love and justice for immigrants, the poor, and all who live on the margins of all societies of all times.

According to Delgado and Stefancic, the basic tenets of CRT include the following:

1. The belief that racism is ordinary: "Racism is ordinary, not aberrational—'normal science,' the normal way society does business, the common, everyday experience of most people of color in this country."[5]

2. Interest convergence or material determinism: "Because racism advances the interests of both white elites (materially) and working-class Caucasians

---

4. An interesting wrinkle in the Marxist critique of CRT is that one prominent Marxist scholar has actually argued that CRT and Marxism are necessarily opposed. See Cole, *Critical Race Theory and Education*.

5. Delgado and Stefancic, *Critical Race Theory*, 8.

(psychically), large segments of society have little incentive to eradicate it."[6]

3. The social construction thesis: "Race and races are products of social thought and relations. Not objective, inherent, or fixed, they correspond to no biological or genetic reality."[7]

4. The voice of color thesis: "Because of their different histories and experiences with oppression, black, American Indian, Asian, and Latina/o writers and thinkers may be able to communicate to their white counterparts matters that the whites are unlikely to know."[8]

Beyond these basic tenets, other central themes of CRT include intersectionality, legal indeterminacy, white privilege, whiteness as property, revisionist history, and legal storytelling.

In her classic article, "Whiteness as Property," Cheryl Harris persuasively argues that "whiteness" developed as a legal property interest in US history and served as the basis for the inequitable distribution of socioeconomic and political benefits. Those who possessed whiteness in the eyes of the law were viewed as full human beings and were entitled to citizenship, the right to vote, property ownership, and so forth. On the other hand, those excluded from the possession of whiteness by the courts were legally defined as "black" and viewed as chattel. According to Harris, "Slavery as a system of property facilitated the merger of white identity and property. . . . Whiteness was the characteristic, the attribute, the property of free human beings."[9]

6. Delgado and Stefancic, *Critical Race Theory*, 9.
7. Delgado and Stefancic, *Critical Race Theory*, 9.
8. Delgado and Stefancic, *Critical Race Theory*, 11.
9. Harris, "Whiteness as Property," 1721.

To build on Harris's analysis, one might also say that British and other European imperial powers misappropriated Christianity as an aspect of their legal property interest in whiteness. In their view, Christianity was their property, and to be Christian was to be white. They alone held the institutional and theological keys to the kingdom of God, and that justified their colonial expansion over Africa, Asia, the Americas, and the Near East. According to the Doctrine of Discovery, Europeans could violently seize the lands of non-Christian ethnic groups for purposes of religious conversion. Indeed, people of color throughout the globe were considered "fortunate" to receive the salvation of their souls in exchange for the small price of their lands and enslavement.

From the springboard of the Doctrine of Discovery surfaced a slate of perverted religious doctrines used to justify European colonial expansion well into the twentieth century. These far-fetched theological doctrines included, for example, syncretistic Aristotelian notions of "natural slavery," Manifest Destiny, mark of Cain theology, segregationist tower of Babel theology, and manipulated Kuyperian notions of sphere sovereignty, which were used to justify South African apartheid. At the core of all these twisted theologies was the implicit belief that Christianity belonged fundamentally to Europeans and their colonial descendants. As a consequence, the institutions of Christianity—individual congregations, denominational hierarchies, schools of theological education, and theology—were their property as well. In exchange for the proclamation of a Eurocentric gospel and the spiritual salvation of those they conquered and colonized, they could rule both heaven and earth—or so they thought.

Today, very few would make the bold claim that Christianity is the property of whites alone. After all, Christianity is on the decline in Europe and among whites in America.

Moreover, the Christian faith is experiencing rapid growth in Latin America, Asia, and Africa and is holding strong among Latinas/os, African Americans, and Asian Americans in the United States. The numerical trajectory of global Christianity among non-whites is not contested. At the same time, however, the institutional structures of Christianity in the United States remain firmly white. As in earlier times of de jure segregation, white male leadership continues to dominate individual congregations, religious denominations, publishing houses, seminaries, and Christian colleges and universities. I do not doubt that the vast majority of these leaders possess good will and in true sincerity do not harbor explicit racism. Some, in fact, hold a profound sense of racial consciousness and are aware of their white privilege. For many, however, their limited cultural lens does not allow them to see that the institutions of Christianity in America are still perceived by non-whites as largely the "property" of whites. These racial disparities, moreover, perpetuate the alienation of millions of Christians of color in the United States.

In light of these historical and contemporary misrepresentations of Christianity as a racist religion, I have found CRT helpful as a bridge for witnessing and evangelism. Just as John used the Greek concept of the *logos* as a bridge to share about Jesus with his Greco-Roman audience, and as Paul connected with his hearers at the Areopagus by citing Greek philosophers and poets (Acts 17), so have I been able to share the gospel by using CRT as a cultural bridge to connect with thousands who would have never darkened the door of a church. As a follower of Jesus, I am greatly intrigued by the truths in CRT that comport with the teachings of the Bible. Of course, not everything in CRT is in alignment, but many of the big tenets of CRT line up squarely with the teachings of Jesus and Scripture. Since all truth is God's truth, this does not surprise me at all.

For the sake of illustration, I will offer two examples of the alignment between CRT and the teachings of the Bible, which will both receive comprehensive treatment in later chapters. The first example involves the CRT tenet "Racism is ordinary" and the biblical corollary of sinful human nature expressed through prejudice and fractured human relationships. The second pertains to the CRT concept of community cultural wealth and its parallel concept, "the glory and honor of the nations," found in Revelation 21:26.

The first major tenet of CRT—racism is ordinary—means that racism is an ordinary part of everyday life for people of color in the United States. We experience racism on a regular basis as we go about our daily lives. We feel it in our one-on-one interactions with people, and in big and small ways. As demonstrated by the stories of Angelica and John, and by my own story, racism shows up on an institutional level too—in our schools, hospitals, courtrooms, and political institutions and, unfortunately, even in some of our churches, seminaries, and ministries.

In fact, this idea of racism being "ordinary" and "just the way it is" lines up exactly with a biblical worldview. From the standpoint of the Bible, sin is ordinary. It is our natural bent, apart from God's transformative work in our hearts and lives. As the apostle Paul states, "For all have sinned and fall short of the glory of God, and all are justified freely by his grace through the redemption that came by Christ Jesus" (Rom. 3:23–24). And prejudice and racism are two of the ugliest types of sin. They violate the sacred biblical truth that all people are equal in God's sight because all people are made equally in God's image. Prejudice says, "My culture reflects the image of God more than yours; my people are better because your people are 'criminals, rapists, drug dealers, and uneducated.'" Racism says, "Because my people are culturally superior to yours, I will create laws and policies and will structure society in a way that privileges 'my people.' I will make sure that 'your people' have little to no access to these same privileges and benefits because you are culturally inferior and don't really belong."

Another biblical analog from CRT is that of community cultural wealth. CRT scholars Tara Yosso and Danny Solórzano developed the concept of community cultural wealth in the context of urban educational studies. As will be discussed further in chapter 1, Yosso and Solórzano challenge the traditional educational literature that claims that Latino students are culturally deficient. Instead, they argue that Latino students bring unique forms of community cultural wealth to their K–12 and university educations that are distinct from, but not inferior to, the social capital of white students. Building on this approach, Lindsay Pérez Huber has found that "spiritual capital" is a major component of the community cultural wealth of undocumented student activists. Her interviews with "Dreamers"[10] reveal that faith served as critical "spiritual capital" for their educational success.[11]

Similarly, sacred Scripture teaches that every ethnic group possesses God-given community cultural wealth. In the book of Revelation, John calls this wealth the "glory and honor of

10. The term *Dreamer* is used to refer to undocumented college and university students who were brought by undocumented parents to the United States as children, many of whom were valedictorians or at the top of their high school graduating classes. They persevere through many socioeconomic challenges to pursue their university education and have high hopes for their futures and those of their families.

11. Yosso and Solórzano, "Conceptualizing a Critical Race Theory"; Pérez Huber, "Challenging Racist Nativist Framing."

the nations," which he says "will be brought into [the New Jerusalem]" (Rev. 21:26). The word translated into English as "glory" can also be translated as "treasure" or "wealth." A plausible reading of this passage is that after Jesus returns and makes all things new, the cultural treasure and wealth of every ethnic group of the world will be brought into the New Jerusalem forever. In fact, brown and black churches have been repositories of such diverse glory and honor for more than four centuries, and the burgeoning global and immigrant churches likewise offer an embarrassment of cultural and spiritual riches for the benefit of the entire body of Christ. We should start living into this wonderful reality now! Far too often, people of color are forced to leave their own God-given cultural treasure and wealth outside of white ministries and church doors in order to find acceptance. This is why millions are fleeing the evangelical church and parachurch ministries today. Though God does not have ethnic favorites, neither is God color-blind. Nor should we be.

I (Jeff) am the child of immigrants from Taiwan. My father grew up in a rural farming village as the son of the local apothecary. He would study Western medicine and then immigrate to the United States to complete his residency and practice family medicine and surgery in rural Oklahoma. As with his father before him, the local community relied on him for care. My father returned to Taiwan during his residency to marry my mother, and she joined him in the United States to start an entirely new life in a strange land. Though the only Asian family in a town of three thousand, we enjoyed the hospitality and kindness of neighbors, friends, and even my father's patients. Together, my parents carried and imparted the treasure and wealth that shapes how I see the world and how I conduct myself in it, and I seek to pass this wealth and treasure on to the next generation, my children.

As a child, I saw race as differences in cultural values, extracurricular activities (or lack thereof), and foods. Sometimes I saw it through the lens of the racist epithets that were directed at me in the hall at school. However, it was the 1980s—the same decade in which racial resentment over the rise of the Japanese auto industry led two Detroit autoworkers to murder Vincent Chin, a Chinese American draftsman. My awareness that things were amiss would grow. From the back seat of our family car, I remember seeing a broken-down vehicle being towed with a sign on the back that read, "Jap is crap!" Later, when we had moved to Tulsa, the Chinese church I attended was spray-painted with a red swastika and the words "Gooks Die!" In college, I would take an elective course on Asian Americans and the law from the assistant attorney general of the state of Michigan, Roland Hwang. I was a chemistry major, so this was to be my first exposure to Asian American studies. In fact, I could barely grasp the significance of the conference call the class had with Fred Korematsu, who had brought a lawsuit over Japanese internment against the US government. The case went to the Supreme Court in 1944.

As my sense of belonging to the wider Asian American community grew, so did my calling to ministry. In the 1990s and early 2000s, as the second-generation children of the post-1965 wave of Asian immigrants reached college age, Asian American Christian students began to form Bible studies and student groups. Employed by InterVarsity Christian Fellowship after college, I became the first Asian American staff member of the Chinese Christian Fellowship at the University of Michigan (now renamed Asian InterVarsity). It was here that I explored Asian American racial awareness more deeply. I began to look for biblical and theological resources that were distinct from the kinds of diversity training I received from the university as a residence hall adviser. I wanted to help the students I worked with appreciate and enjoy the riches of Asian American Christian distinctiveness. This desire became critically urgent when a Chinese American friend lost his struggle for mental health, taking his own life. I would learn from a psychologist serving as a special appointee to the Office of the Vice President for Student Affairs that many institutions of higher education had yet to take Asian American student needs—including mental health needs—seriously. I realized then that if R1 institutions—universities with high levels of research—with their massive athletics budgets did not have culturally appropriate resources, then the situation in the local church was going to be a serious problem. I realized also that the church lagged far behind the academy in articulating, discussing, and acting on the needs of people of color—that no one from the ecclesial world was coming to help.

This compelled me to pursue pastoral training and theological study where I would eventually encounter CRT. In my doctoral program, I enlisted Robert's expert guidance to broaden my race and ethnic studies readings while I continued to steep myself in theology and ethics. While simultaneously working in ministry alongside young adults of color *and* reading some of the original writings in critical race theory, I immediately began to see the relevant overlaps between CRT and Christian theology for ministry. In fact, at this point you have seen from Robert's reflections that Christians can view some of the key ideas within CRT through traditional biblical and theological lenses and themes. Why, then, all the fuss? More specifically, why has CRT been deemed "incompatible" with some doctrinal systems and entirely "unbiblical" by some critics?

From the listening I have tried to do, my sense has been that one's posture toward other academic disciplines makes a big difference. This book is our attempt to model a way of engaging an academic discipline (CRT) by integrating Christian faith and theology. Someone who wishes to "take captive every thought to make it obedient to Christ" (2 Cor. 10:5) must avoid unfair oversimplifications and false dichotomies. There are historical examples in which integration of Christian theology and other disciplines has caused alarm for some Christians. As Christianity grappled with the discipline of psychology, for example, "integration" was proposed in the 1940s and 1950s. But some found the tensions with psychology's secularity too problematic, so the "biblical counseling" movement emerged in the 1970s. There are many related examples: the tensions endure between theology and philosophy, theology and sociology, theology and science, and so on. However, all people—including Christians—in some way benefit daily from insights in all these fields. Furthermore, Christians in the workplace, scholars, clergy, activists, and students work *coram deo*—that is, before God—in all these fields and their associated industries. So instead of compatible/incompatible, endorse/renounce, or accept/reject binaries, we have chosen to hold the tensions and point to ways that biblical theology can help us frame some of the key ideas in CRT. If someone decides that the tensions are too great to hold, I hope they come to that decision *after* having grappled in good faith.

With this approach in mind, I believe that it is possible to understand some Christian traditions to have engaged in a kind of critical social analysis well before CRT. Certainly, many Christian communities of color (which may or may not be invested in this admittedly theoretical conversation) have already organized and operationalized their collective memories of racism and understanding of systems and structures that work against them in order to stand firm in the gospel. I am personally more concerned about those who would lean into a declaration that CRT is "antithetical to the Bible" and what such a declaration might mean for their fellowship with Christian traditions and communities that have taught and believed differently from them for decades and even centuries. What might it mean for ecumenicity and interdenominational cooperation against racial injustice?

The difference in responses couldn't be more dramatic or pastorally significant. On March 16, 2021, eight people were shot and killed in two separate spas in Atlanta, Georgia. Six of these victims were Asian American women. (Their names have been released elsewhere, but I have withheld them here as I continue to process the complexities of how and whether naming victims might shame or honor them and their families at this time and at this particular intersection of racial and sexual violence.) The mass murderer, a twenty-one-year-old white man, took responsibility. The church where he is a member issued a formal statement that takes pains to clarify that the church does not believe that the victims should be blamed.

However, in the course of making that clarification, the statement reads, "He alone is responsible for his evil actions and desires. . . . These actions are the result of a sinful heart and depraved mind for which [he] is completely responsible. . . . Each person is responsible for his or her own sin."[12] The total failure to take any responsibility for the shaping of this man's heart and mind is endemic to the "accountable freewill

---

12. Scott Barkley, "Georgia Church Condemns 'Extreme and Wicked' Actions of Member, Initiates Church Discipline," *Baptist Press*, March 19, 2021, https://www.baptistpress.com/resource-library/news/georgia-church-condemns-extreme-and-wicked-actions-of-member-initiates-church-discipline/.

individualistic" doctrine of sin in which we are not necessarily our siblings' keepers. Doctrine, theology, and ecclesial institutions play no role and therefore require no redress in such a selectively biblicist logic. It should be clear that this relatively novel commitment to Western individualism functions as a commonsense apologetic for inaction.

Over the past several years, as anti-Asian racism has become increasingly lethal, I have pictured my own parents and friends being targeted for their racialized vulnerability. I also picture the faces of many other "aunties" and "uncles," both known and unknown to me, that I have seen victimized—one precious "auntie" I loved, murdered brutally. As I have sojourned through this lonely trauma, I recall what CRT has elaborated. I could have settled into the mistaken notion that these incidents are isolated, or that they're the province of a lunatic fringe. I could have given quarter to the inability of clergy to call this what it is—a racist pattern and live threat. I could have indulged antiblack and antibrown sentiment that tells Asian Americans that cultivating proximity to whiteness is safety.

To the contrary, CRT enables us to identify the ways in which certain theologies, in an ill-fated attempt to same-ify and flatten what God has made beautifully diverse, result in the most polite, psychological, and physical death dealing. In believing, for example, that racism is ordinary, I no longer have to internalize the lie that the Asian American experience of racism is a figment of a hypersensitive imagination—as we have been told for decades. In order to condemn racism in all its forms, one must understand the novel, viral strains of racism that are emerging. CRT is actually indispensable in this regard because it, too, organizes and operationalizes the collective memories of racism and understanding of systems and structures that work against Asian Americans.

As I write, I realize that I am addressing the percentage of clergy and church leaders who are still discerning their way through this theological, theoretical, praxiological, and pastoral jumble. Simplistic dismissals of CRT are alluring amid tension and turbulence at this time. Those dismissals offer only false peace by resolving the cognitive dissonance between the desire for ease and a longing for justice. Hence, I want to be quick to point out that an academic movement does not cry out for your attention in the same way that communities racked by racial injustice do. So as I write this, a single word rises in my spirit: neighbor. As you are driven by love of neighbor, I trust that you, dear readers, will seek to understand "racism in all its forms," including those forms articulated by CRT. I trust that you will subject your study of CRT and your very selves to the lordship of Jesus Christ as we meet him by the Holy Spirit in Scripture read alongside the rest of the body of Christ around the globe. As you study in community, I trust that you will be diligent to grant greater honor to those from whom it has been withheld.

We believe that a faithful and constructive engagement with CRT illuminates significant overlaps with Christian theology. In fact, we have organized the chapters by using a classic and simple biblical narrative schema, into which some of the themes of CRT conveniently fall: creation, fall, redemption, and consummation. It is worth articulating that the choice of these four themes is not a commentary on the many ways that theologians and biblical scholars have worked to thematize the drama of Scripture—including those who have helpfully sought to correct the supersessionist omission of Israel as a major "act" in the drama. Rather, it is our finding that theology-ready themes in CRT include (but are not limited to) community cultural wealth, the ordinariness of racism, race-consciousness, and beloved community. This way of submitting an academic concept to the scrutiny of Scripture will highlight areas of continuity and discontinuity, consonance and dissonance. Where there is consonance, it is our intention to demonstrate the ways in which CRT contributes to the ministry of churches and organizations pursuing racial justice.

Chapter 1 explains how community cultural wealth, a CRT concept deployed in educational scholarship, resonates with the theology of creation in the image of God. Instead of a "deficit view," which has been used to paint student populations in a negative light, educators—and Christians— can look at God's children as bearers of the image of God. In fact, education scholars using CRT are keen to include spirituality as one of the assets (or forms of "capital") in their positive view of students. This is the kind of view of students one might expect from someone informed and in-spired by John's vision in Revelation (which resonates with Isa. 60). In Revelation, John's multicultural vision of the kingdom of God includes the "glory and honor of the na-tions" streaming into the presence of God as treasures from the peoples of the earth. "Brown Theology" is introduced as a way in which cultural treasure shapes the spiritual lives and practices of Latin Americans and US Latinas/os.

Chapter 2 wades into the contentious discussion of CRT in the media and in the pews. Somewhere near the center of the ideological disagreement is the doctrine of sin. How one understands the nature and scope of sin, it is argued, has a direct impact on one's view of the nature and scope of racism. A narrow view of *sin as act* and the relatively recent innovation of individualist culpability thinking are not the only options for a doctrine of sin—either in the his-tory of Christian theology or in the global church. Widening our understanding of racism, critical race theorist Eduardo

Bonilla-Silva (and other critical race theorists) directs us away from a misplaced focus on attitudes and beliefs. As the scope widens, racism is understood to be as ordinary, innovative, cunning, and wily as sin because of the fall. Hence, engaging racism in all its forms for the sake of the gospel benefits from the incisive critique that CRT offers.

They are not necessarily new forms of resistance to racism, but CRT describes some of the tools in use. Chapter 3 uses institutions of Christian higher education as an example of the ways in which the tools of CRT can make a redemptive difference. The voice of color thesis encourages students and faculty of color that they are in the best position to understand their own racialized experiences and needs on campus. At best, inattention to these voices leaves student development professionals ill-equipped to do their work. Worse, the dismissal of voices of color leaves students and faculty on the margins of the university of community. In response, Robert offers his own "counterstory" to bring to light his experience in Christian higher education. As a part of his experience, color blindness is revisited at length as a major challenge in the way institutions approach the populations they serve. Despite these challenges, many are the hands and hopeful are the efforts that are changing the landscape.

While we believe CRT contributes to the redemptive work of justice, there is a distinctive contribution that Christian theology makes as well. The final chapter explores the difference that Christian hope in the consummation of all things makes for the ethics of those pursuing racial justice. Many activists now use the term *beloved community* that was popularized by Rev. Dr. Martin Luther King Jr. The distinctively theological aspirations of beloved community have inspired and sustained Christian communities for social action. While critical race theorists work hard to reimagine and work toward a just and equitable society, we are convinced that Christian eschatology is a significantly different vision. In fact, because of the cross of Christ, the Christian tradition can access a kind of redemptive disruption of its own.

We conclude with what we hope are pastoral words for our readers from various vantage points and locations in the current fracas. Some are struggling to endure. Too often our suffering is unheard and disbelieved, eventually forcing many of us into a brutal kind of exile that takes a serious spiritual and emotional toll. Others are working out of their good will, contending with challenging congregational cultures. Here we express our hope for the churches and leaders we know and love.

Both of us see more at stake here than just the fair treatment of an obscure academic discipline. We are mindful of Paul's strong words to Timothy about "foolish, ignorant controversies" (2 Tim. 2:23 ESV). The controversy surrounding CRT is about more than rhetorical wrangling. The many faces of racism in the church are and have been both exclusive and repulsive. Racism has set up barriers to meaningful fellowship, and it has sent many to wander ecclesial and spiritual deserts. We hope that this book will be an occasion for Christians to look together at a shared future for the sake of the gospel.

# 1

# Creation

## Community Cultural Wealth and the Glory and Honor of the Nations

### Introduction

At a recent family gathering to celebrate my aunt's eightieth birthday, she shared with me (Robert) about her experiences growing up in the public school system of El Paso, Texas, in the 1950s. Although the Romeros had lived in the El Paso-Juarez-Chihuahua region for hundreds of years, before Texas was ever part of the United States, they immigrated to El Paso in the 1950s in the long wake of the economic disruptions caused by the Mexican Revolution. As we reminisced over old family photos, my aunt revealed something deeply disturbing about her elementary school experience: Anglo teachers used to tape her mouth shut whenever she spoke in Spanish.

Although de jure segregation of Mexican American students in Texas was outlawed in the case of *Delgado v. Bastrop ISD* (1948), the racist attitudes that fueled educational segregation continued to manifest themselves, perhaps unsurprisingly, several years later, when my aunts, uncles, and father attended the public schools of El Paso. In fact, notwithstanding the official end to legalized segregation in the *Brown v. Board of Education* case of 1954, the state of Texas continued the segregation of Mexican and African American students from white students through a legal loophole well into the 1970s. Since Mexicans were legally defined as "white," Texas officials argued, the constitutional requirements of integration could be fulfilled by placing "white" Mexicans into schools with black students, leaving predominantly white Anglo schools intact. Unfortunately, similar racist educational policies would also later follow my family members into the middle schools and high schools of East Los Angeles, but with higher stakes. My father, for example, was tracked into low-achieving classes and, with his brother, was drafted to fight in Vietnam.

As mentioned previously, as a student in the 1970s and '80s, I experienced racist attitudes ranging from slurs to educational tracking to police profiling. I could share many other examples of micro- and macroaggressions from my ensuing years in college, in graduate school, and even later as a tenured professor at UCLA.

Fast-forward to the present moment: I remember being shocked when my son wasn't placed in the middle school honors classes he deserved to be in. Despite having received perfect scores on his standardized tests and having graduated as the top student of his diverse and high-performing elementary school, he was placed by the school counselor in only a single honors class. Was it implicit bias? I'll never know for sure, but you can probably imagine the generational racial trauma that resurfaced for me while I reviewed his schedule. You can probably also imagine my response.

The types of personal and structural racism that I, and my family before me, endured in the public school system have been well documented by education scholars for decades. Moreover, the legacy of such explicitly racist educational practices has carried over into the structures of contemporary education in various forms, such as the underfunding of urban schools, the emerging trend of resegregation in secondary and higher education, tracking, anti-immigrant state laws targeting undocumented youth, and the school-to-prison pipeline.

According to data on the Chicana/o educational pipeline, moreover, of every hundred Latina/o elementary school students in the United States, forty-six graduate from high school and only eight graduate with a baccalaureate degree. Of these eight college graduates, only two will go on to receive a graduate or professional degree, and fewer than one will eventually receive a doctorate.[1] For those with eyes to see and ears to hear, a mountain of data establishes the present existence of educational inequality in the United States. Using CRT in education as a unique framework, Chicana/o educational scholars such as Daniel Solórzano, Patricia Gándara, Dolores Delgado Bernal, Tara Yosso, David García, and Lindsay Pérez Huber have produced monumental interdisciplinary research and theories to help solve and explain such educational inequality. According to pioneering Chicana/o education scholars Solórzano and Yosso, a CRT

1. Yosso and Solórzano, "Leaks in the Chicana and Chicano Educational Pipeline," 1.

framework in education can be used in the following five ways:

1. To center the research focus on race, racism, and the intersections of multiple forms of oppression
2. To challenge dominant ideologies imbedded in educational theory and practice
3. To recognize the significance of experiential knowledge and utilize this knowledge in our research
4. To utilize interdisciplinary perspectives
5. To guide our work with a commitment to racial and social justice[2]

In the words of Pérez Huber, "Collectively, these strategies allow educational researchers to center the experiences of People of Color and reveal the ways racism and other forms of subordination mediate our educational trajectories." Pérez Huber also asserts that CRT helps us to challenge the racist, nativist framing that has guided traditional educational theory—and, I might add, that has blossomed in the United States and within many swaths of the US evangelical church—over the past decade as a consequence of the Tea Party and Make America Great Again movements.[3]

Yosso's pathbreaking CRT framework of community cultural wealth is helpful for understanding both the historical and the temporary trends of racism within the US educational system, as well as for transforming the process of schooling in the United States. Community cultural wealth rejects a "deficit" view of communities of color as sites of cultural poverty

2. This list is quoted from Pérez Huber, "Challenging Racist Nativist Framing," 708.
3. Pérez Huber, "Challenging Racist Nativist Framing," 708, 711.

and disadvantage; instead, it emphasizes and learns from the array of cultural knowledge, skills, abilities, and contacts that socially marginalized groups bring to the education process and that often go overlooked and unrecognized.[4]

As we'll also see, the CRT framework of community cultural wealth has a powerful biblical analog in the concept of the "glory and honor of the nations" found in Revelation 21:26–27. The biblical framework of the glory and honor of the nations, in turn, offers compelling theological tools for understanding current racial and cultural divisions within the US church, as well as for transforming ecclesial models of the twenty-first century to reflect a God-given, biblical diversity and cultural identity.

## Community Cultural Wealth

Traditional educational approaches toward Latina/o students and other students of color have taken a cultural "deficit" view.[5] In earlier eras, this cultural deficit approach stated explicitly that Latino students were culturally—and even biologically—inferior to white students in ways that hindered Latino students' educational advancement. Here are some examples of these kinds of assumptions: Latinos are lazy because they come from tropical environments. They are all on welfare and are a drain on the system. They are criminals, rapists, and drug dealers. They don't value education. Most Latino dads abandon their families. And the list goes on. Since Latino culture was viewed as the problem, educational policies therefore aimed at cultural erasure, at "Americanizing" Latino students and assimilating them

4. Yosso, "Whose Culture Has Capital?," 69.
5. Yosso, "Whose Culture Has Capital?," 69, 75–76.

completely into white, middle-class American norms and values. This in turn led to invidious racial practices, such as taping the mouths of students, as has already been discussed; the creation of segregated "Mexican schools" throughout California, Texas, and the Southwest; the tracking of Latino students into vocational education classes and low-paying "Mexican" jobs; and the exclusion of Latino students from college-prep courses.

In more recent times, cultural deficit approaches have morphed into (usually) more polite expressions. Drawing from the theoretical insights of Pierre Bourdieu, some say that Latino educational attainment is hampered because Latino students lack the social and cultural capital of the white American upper and middle classes. White middle-class culture is viewed as "wealthy" and is the standard by which all others are judged. As a result, Latinos and other students of color are seen as culturally "poor."[6] The recently retracted comments of Christian evangelist Josh McDowell to the American Association of Christian Counselors reflect this cultural deficit approach: "I do not believe Blacks, African Americans, and many other minorities have equal opportunity. Why? Most of them grew up in families where there is not a big emphasis on education, security—you can do anything you want. You can change the world. If you work hard, you will make it. So many African Americans don't have those privileges like I was brought up with."[7]

Viewed in this cultural deficit light, assimilation is the solution for the perceived cultural deprivation of communities

6. Yosso, "Whose Culture Has Capital?," 70, 76.
7. Bob Smietana, "Christian Author Josh McDowell Steps Away from Ministry after Comments about Black, Minority Families," *Religion News Service*, September 19, 2021, https://religionnews.com/2021/09/19/christian-author-josh-mcdowell-denounces-crt-says-black-and-minority-families-dont-value-hard-work-and-education/.

of color. Guided by these assumptions, moreover, the goal of K–12 education is to pour white middle-class culture and values into the empty and cracked cultural jars of Latinos through a banking method of education.[8] Stated crudely, the goal is to turn students of color into white, middle-class Americans.

In response to such cultural deficit approaches, Yosso and Solórzano developed the concept of community cultural wealth in the context of urban educational studies.[9] Instead of approaching Latino educational achievement in terms of cultural deficit models, which depict Latino students as deficient insofar as they are unlike white suburban students, Yosso and Solórzano argue that scholarly analysis should begin with an understanding of the unique community cultural wealth possessed by Chicanos/Latinos. According to Yosso in her classic essay "Whose Culture Has Capital? A Critical Race Theory Discussion of Community Cultural Wealth," "A CRT lens can 'see' that Communities of Color nurture cultural wealth through at least 6 forms of capital such as aspirational, navigational, social, linguistic, familial, and resistant capital."[10]

In turn, enhanced educational achievement is best cultivated by drawing from and building on the community cultural wealth that students of color bring with them from their families and communities into the classroom. As I will argue, community cultural wealth is a gift that God gives to people of every ethnic group (Rev. 21:26), and one of the gravest sins of the United States over the past four hundred years has been the idol of American exceptionalism, which claims that the cultural glory and honor of Anglo-Americans is superior to all others.

8. Yosso, "Whose Culture Has Capital?," 75.
9. Yosso and Solórzano, "Conceptualizing a Critical Race Theory," 127–34.
10. Yosso, "Whose Culture Has Capital?," 77.

Briefly, let's look at each of Yosso's six forms of capital within community cultural wealth. *Aspirational* capital refers to the resiliency of students and their families and their ability to maintain hopes and dreams of advancement in the face of various socioeconomic and political barriers and challenges. *Navigational* capital refers to the inner resources, social competencies, and cultural strategies that urban students develop in order to survive and thrive. *Social* capital refers to broader networks of people and community resources, such as mutual aid societies, which are created to pool and share resources so that members of the community can transcend the challenges of daily life. *Linguistic* capital includes the bilingualism that many Latinx students bring to their education and reflects the distinct language and communications skills nurtured in their family and community contexts. *Familial* capital refers to the diverse forms of cultural wealth and knowledge cultivated among kin—both immediate and extended family units—"that carry a sense of community history, memory, and cultural intuition."[11] For example, our *familias* instruct us how to go beyond our personal needs in order to care for others of the community and provide a reservoir of shared resources. Finally, *resistant* capital refers to the verbal and nonverbal lessons that minority students learn from their families and communities about how to value themselves and resist structures of racism and patriarchy.[12] In my own life, for example, I learned how to resist the racism that I experience in professional and educational settings through observing my father, who helped desegregate the Los Angeles public schools in the 1970s.

11. Yosso, "Whose Culture Has Capital?," 78–79.
12. Yosso, "Whose Culture Has Capital?," 79–80.

Building upon Yosso's community cultural wealth framework, Pérez Huber has found that "spiritual capital" is also a major component of the community cultural wealth of female students who identify as undocumented, low-income, and of Mexican descent.[13] After twenty in-depth interviews with "Dreamers" at a major public university, Pérez Huber found that faith serves as important spiritual capital for educational success:[14] "Spiritual capital can be understood as a set of resources and skills rooted in a spiritual connection to a reality greater than oneself. Spiritual capital can encompass religious, indigenous, and ancestral beliefs and practices learned from one's family, community, and inner self. Thus, spirituality in its many forms can provide a sense of hope and faith."[15]

For the interview participants, faith (implicitly Christian faith) served as a source of strength and resiliency in the face of multiple socioeconomic barriers. In the words of one student, Brenda: "I think I'm a woman with great faith. So I really trust God, he has great plans for me. But sometimes I feel like, 'Where am I going to work after [graduation]?' Although there's days I really, really want to give up, . . . I can't give up."[16]

For Daria, a second-year psychology major, faith was part of her early formation and allowed her both to overcome the obstacles of her life and to find redemptive purpose and peace in the midst of them:

> Religion has always been a very big part of my life since I was young. . . . For me it's always been a source of strength,

13. Pérez Huber, "Challenging Racist Nativist Framing," 712, 721.
14. Pérez Huber, "Challenging Racist Nativist Framing," 713.
15. Pérez Huber, "Challenging Racist Nativist Framing," 721.
16. Pérez Huber, "Challenging Racist Nativist Framing," 722.

a source of hope, a source of faith, a source of positivity in my life. You know, everybody goes through their struggles . . . and there [are] times when you're down, and I've learned to think positively ahead . . . to think that I'm here for a reason, that all this that I've gone through is for a reason. God has always been there for me, to help me get through. There's no problem in my life so big that I've never been able to overcome thus far. Thank God. Whether it was fear of going to college, fear of how I'm going to pay for college, fear of "how am I going to pass that class?" Fear of anything. I've learned to not stress out so much because of that confidence, that I know that God has always put me through it. So for me it's a big part of who I am. It's given me a lot of confidence, a lot of . . . what's it called? Peace.[17]

As we will see, as with the Athenian altar to the unknown God of Acts 17, these powerful student testimonies of spiritual capital, together with Yosso's community cultural wealth model, point the field of CRT to a knowledge of Jesus Christ and a biblical understanding of cultural diversity when followed to their logical conclusion.

Drawing on the important theories of my colleagues Yosso, Solórzano, and Pérez Huber, I have argued elsewhere that spiritual capital is not just a feature of contemporary Latina/o community cultural wealth but that it has been a distinguishing marker of the diverse Latina/o community since Latin American colonial times. "From Juan Diego to Guáman Poma de Ayala, Garcilaso de la Vega el Inca, and Las Casas; to the iconic civil rights movement of Dolores Huerta and César Chávez, to the Sanctuary Movement of the 1980s, and the contemporary immigration reform movement, spiritual capital has been a central component of

17. Pérez Huber, "Challenging Racist Nativist Framing," 722.

Latina/o community cultural wealth."[18] For more than five hundred years, spiritual capital has empowered Latinas/os to contest racial and social injustice in Latin America and the United States as part of the Brown Church.[19] The Brown Church has been a repository of five centuries of God-given spiritual capital and community cultural wealth.

As we will see, however, from a biblical perspective, community cultural wealth is not limited to the realm of social justice struggle. Nor is it limited to particular ethnic groups. Rather, as described by John in the book of Revelation, all ethnic groups possess God-given "glory and honor," or community cultural treasure and wealth, which is of eternal value and is a defining feature of the multicultural kingdom of God.

## The Book of Revelation and the Glory and Honor of the Nations

> After this I looked, and there before me was a great multitude that no one could count, *from every nation, tribe, people and language*, standing before the throne and before the Lamb. They were wearing white robes and were holding palm branches in their hands. And they cried out in a loud voice:
>
> > "Salvation belongs to our God,
> > who sits on the throne,
> > and to the Lamb."
>
> > Revelation 7:9–10, emphasis added

18. Romero, *Brown Church*, 10–11.
19. The Brown Church may be formally defined as "a prophetic ecclesial community of Latinas/os which has contested racial and social injustice in Latin America and the United States for the past 500 years. As such, 'Brown Church' is a multivalent category, encompassing ethnic, historical, theological, spiritual, and socio-political dimensions." Romero, *Brown Church*, 11.

I did not see a temple in the city, because the Lord God Almighty and the Lamb are its temple. . . . *The glory and honor of the nations* will be brought into it. *Nothing impure will ever enter* it, nor will anyone who does what is shameful or deceitful, but only those whose names are written in the Lamb's book of life.

Revelation 21:22, 26–27, emphasis added

The framework of community cultural wealth finds its corollary in the book of Revelation. The racial tensions examined by CRT, moreover, find their parallel in the ways the early church and the seven churches of Asia Minor wrestled with understanding the proper relationship between ethnic culture and the kingdom of God. According to historical theologian Justo González, the book of Revelation can, in fact, be characterized as its author's "multicultural challenge" and as an exercise in cultural crossing.[20] The book of Revelation may be viewed as John's attempt to make sense of the multicultural reality—present and future—of the kingdom of God. In light of John's use of unpolished Greek, together with his frequent paraphrases of the Hebrew Bible (rather than quotations from the Greek Septuagint, which was also available to him), González and others speculate that John was an immigrant—a Palestinian Jew thrust into exile and living among the seven churches of the Roman province of Asia, modern western Turkey.[21] Scholarly consensus places John's letter to the seven churches of Ephesus, Smyrna, Pergamum, Thyatira, Sardis, Philadelphia, and Laodicea at around AD 95, toward the latter part of the reign of Roman emperor Domitian (AD 81–96).[22] It is

20. González, *For the Healing of the Nations*, 59, 69.
21. González, *For the Healing of the Nations*, 58–59, 63.
22. Gorman, *Reading Revelation Responsibly*, 37, 39. Gunsalus González and González, *Vision at Patmos*, 10.

also believed that the members of these seven churches were mostly Jewish.

One tension experienced by John and other diaspora Jews throughout the Roman Empire involved the cultural integration of gentile converts within the early church. They wondered specifically how the good news of the kingdom of God, which was announced first within an entirely Jewish cultural context, should be translated to all nations as part of the Great Commission (Matt. 28:16–20).[23] Should gentiles be required to become circumcised and follow the traditional law of Moses in order to become part of the church? This would be tantamount to requiring Greek, Roman, and other gentile converts to become culturally Jewish in order to follow Jesus.

We find examples of this specific cultural tension in Paul's letter to the Galatians, as well as in Luke's account of the convening of the Jerusalem Council following the rapid incorporation of gentiles into the diverse church at Antioch. As Luke narrates, "certain people came down from Judea" (Acts 15:1) and taught erroneously that in order to become grafted into the family of God, gentiles must first resign their God-given cultural heritage and adopt the Jewish religious and cultural identity through circumcision and obedience to the entire law of Moses. González asserts that such unwarranted pressure amounted to the first "Aramaic-only movement," akin to modern-day English-only movements in the United States.[24] In response, the Jerusalem Council affirmed the principle that faith in Jesus the Messiah does not require the cultural conversion of gentiles to Jewish ethnicity. Rather, Christianity should be allowed to take unique cultural shape within the diverse ethnic families of the world. In the context

23. González, *For the Healing of the Nations*, 45.
24. González, *For the Healing of the Nations*, 44, 49.

of that earliest church described in the book of Acts, the only specific provisions carried over from the Mosaic law were that gentile believers should "abstain from food polluted by idols, from sexual immorality, from the meat of strangled animals and from blood" (Acts 15:20).

In the book of Revelation, John affirms the bold multicultural position of the Jerusalem Council by offering multiple visions of diverse heavenly worship (Rev. 5:9–10; 7:9–10). Consistent with the teaching of Peter in Acts 10:34–35, John makes it clear that Christ does not play a game of ethnic favoritism, but rather, he gave his life to establish a multicultural kingdom of priests from "every tribe and language and people and nation" to worship and serve God forever and ever (Rev. 5:9). Our diverse ethnic backgrounds are of eternal value to God, and these categories of tribe, language, people, and nation will find eternal fulfillment in the New Jerusalem.

And they sang a new song, saying:

> "You are worthy to take the scroll
>     and to open its seals,
> because you were slain,
>     and with your blood you purchased for God
>     persons *from every tribe and language and people
>         and nation.*
> You have made them to be a kingdom and priests to
>     serve our God,
>     and they will reign on the earth."
>                                        Revelation 5:9–10, emphasis added

Such radical ancient declarations make the book of Revelation one of the greatest multicultural community–forming documents ever written.[25]

25. Gorman, *Reading Revelation Responsibly*, 187.

In addition to the cultural tension related to gentile cultural integration, John and the seven churches of Asia faced major questions related to the propriety of Roman cultural accommodation. For example, how should followers of Jesus negotiate Rome's empire and cultural practices in their daily lives?[26] Was it appropriate for members of the seven churches to embrace Roman imperial nationalism and participate in the pagan system of emperor worship and civil religion in order to maintain their economic and political standing in Roman society?[27]

Because pagan and imperial religion pervaded all aspects of life in ancient Roman society, early Christians could not avoid it. They interacted with Roman paganism at athletic events and rhetorical contests, in the purchasing and eating of meat from pagan temples, through membership in trade guilds, when banking in pagan temples, and in emperor worship and civil religion.[28]

The imperial cult consisted of three main beliefs:

1. Rome is chosen by the gods.
2. Rome and its emperors are agents of the rule, will, and salvation of the gods.
3. In order to benefit from the blessings of salvation, peace, and prosperity offered by the gods, one is required to submit to the imperial rule of Rome and Caesar.

As part of this package of Roman Manifest Destiny, the emperors were worshiped and assigned titles such as "Lord,"

---

26. W. Carter, "Accommodating 'Jezebel' and Withdrawing John," 32.
27. Gorman, *Reading Revelation Responsibly*, 45, 46.
28. Gorman, *Reading Revelation Responsibly*, 44.

"Lord of all," "God," "Son of God," "Lord and God," and "Savior."[29]

When John wrote the book of Revelation, the seven churches—Ephesus, Smyrna, Pergamum, Thyatira, Sardis, Philadelphia, and Laodicea—were enamored with the wealth and power of Rome and were vying to become leading Romanized cities. In particular, the elites of these provincial cities were vying for Roman imperial favor and, according to Bruce Longenecker, were serving as the major conveyors of Roman culture and imperial structures.[30] So that they could receive the economic and political benefits of Rome, they were thoroughly committed to Romanization and competed for the title of "first of the province" or "first of the district."[31] Drawn by the allure of Roman power and prestige, or perhaps even instincts of survival, some Christians also advocated working within the Roman religious, economic, and political system.[32] Chapters 1–3 of Revelation can be characterized as Jesus's critique of five of the seven churches of Asia Minor (all except Smyrna and Philadelphia) for their compromise with the culture of the Roman Empire. Indeed, much of the book of Revelation has been interpreted as a prophetic critique of Rome (symbolized as Babylon) and a warning to Christian believers of all ages against the enchantment of empire and its destructive cultural practices.[33]

According to González, empire even produces a distorted multiculturalism that runs counter to the cultural diversity envisioned by the kingdom of God: "Although Multiculturalism may be an important trait of the very nature of

---

29. Gorman, *Reading Revelation Responsibly*, 53.
30. Longenecker, "Rome, Provincial Cities and the Seven Churches," 282.
31. Longenecker, "Rome, Provincial Cities and the Seven Churches," 287.
32. Longenecker, "Rome, Provincial Cities and the Seven Churches," 284.
33. González, *For the Healing of the Nations*, 65.

the church, . . . it is also an important trait of the powers of evil," because empire draws together "every people, tribe, language and nation" (Rev. 11:9; cf. 13:7; 17:15) into a false type of multiculturalism centered on the pursuit of wealth and power and claims that members of one particular ethnic group possess a "divine destiny" to rule all others.[34] Such false diversity does not take into account the ways in which sin distorts the image of God as uniquely expressed in the ethnic cultures of the world. Also, it does not consider the ways that empire often co-opts cultural diversity to produce ethnic cleansing and destructive notions of racial and cultural exclusivism.[35] In sum, Revelation offers two competing visions of cultural diversity: (1) all nations worshiping before Christ and (2) all nations worshiping before the beast of empire.[36] For Christians of the early church, and of all times, the latter is not an option. John's message to the seven churches about cultural and religious compromise with Rome is clear and unequivocal:

> *"Come out of her, my people,"*
>> so that you will not share in her sins,
>> so that you will not receive any of her plagues;
> for her sins are piled up to heaven,
>> and God has remembered her crimes.
> Give back to her as she has given;
>> pay her back double for what she has done.
>> Pour her a double portion from her own cup.
> Give her as much torment and grief
>> as the glory and luxury she gave herself.

. . . . . . . . . . . . . . . . . . . . . . . . . . . . . . . . .

34. González, *For the Healing of the Nations*, 74–75.
35. González, *For the Healing of the Nations*, 78–79.
36. González, *For the Healing of the Nations*, 111.

> She will be consumed by fire,
> for mighty is the Lord God who judges her.
> Revelation 18:4–8, emphasis added

## The Glory and Honor or "Community Cultural Wealth" of the Nations

So far we have clearly established that John, in the book of Revelation, casts a multicultural vision of the kingdom of God as comprising people from every nation, tribe, people, and language. Understood within John's original historical context of the late first century AD, this vision of ethnic diversity is extraordinary. Revelation 21–22, moreover, adds a layer of hopeful texture to John's previous descriptions. In Revelation 21:26, John declares that the glory and honor of the different ethnic groups of the world will be brought into the New Jerusalem forever. In Revelation 22:2, John adds that "the leaves of the tree [of life] are for the healing of the nations." By God's design and plan, every ethnic group of the world possesses cultural treasure and wealth that is of eternal value, as we will discuss in greater detail below. In the language of Yosso, every ethnic group of the world possesses "community cultural wealth." We will spend eternity partaking of this cultural treasure, offering it up to God in worship and seeking the healing of the ethnic wounds we have received while walking in this broken and fallen world.

In Revelation 21, John offers descriptions and images to help us understand what it will be like after Jesus returns, heaven and earth are reunited, and all things are made new. Some of these images are well trodden in biblical exposition, but two verses in particular—26 and 27—are almost always overlooked, even in most evangelical Bible commentaries.

42

In these verses, John articulates a compelling theology of belonging:

> I did not see a temple in the city, because the Lord God Almighty and the Lamb are its temple. The city does not need the sun or the moon to shine on it, for the glory of God gives it light, and the Lamb is its lamp. The nations will walk by its light, and the kings of the earth will bring their splendor into it. On no day will its gates ever be shut, for there will be no night there. *The glory and honor of the nations* will be brought into it. *Nothing impure will ever enter it*, nor will anyone who does what is shameful or deceitful, but only those whose names are written in the Lamb's book of life. (Rev. 21:22–27, emphasis added)

What is this "glory and honor" that John is speaking of? The Greek word *doxa*, which is translated into English as "glory" in this passage, can also be translated as "treasure" or "wealth." If we understand this word in this light, one way to restate this passage is to say that the treasure or wealth of the different ethnic groups of the world will be brought into the New Jerusalem for eternity. Surely John is not describing literal currency or national government coffers. I believe that he is talking about the cultural treasure or wealth of the different ethnic groups of the world. In the language of Yosso and CRT, we each possess community cultural wealth. This cultural treasure or "glory" is a reflection of the glory of God in and through each of us as God's unique children. God does not make "shithole" countries. We all have equal dignity in God's eyes. By God's design, we each bring distinct cultural glory and honor to the body of Christ as an offering of praise to Jesus—these are signposts that point us to God (Acts 17:26–27) and draw us and the church into deeper understanding and relationship with him.

In my personal reflection, I believe this community cultural wealth includes at least two categories:

1. Tangible aspects of ethnic culture, such as food, music, dance, literature, and architecture
2. The distinct lenses and perspectives that every ethnic group brings to the world and the body of Christ

The first category—food, music, dance, and so forth—is quite obvious. Every ethnic group has its unique forms and flavors. We enjoy this expression of the "glory and honor of the nations" whenever we spend time with friends of a different cultural background, eat at an ethnic restaurant that is outside our norm, visit a museum, listen to world music, attend a concert, or travel abroad. Each time we do these things, we naturally intuit that there is something "glorious" about our experience.

The second category merits more explanation. As I traverse Mexican, Latina/o, Chinese, Asian, Egyptian, German midwestern, and other cultures, I notice that different groups possess distinct lenses, perspectives, and cultural wisdom about Christ, Scripture, and the world. Each uniquely expresses different aspects of God's heart and perspective. I am not arguing for a wishy-washy cultural relativism, nor am I saying that all hermeneutics are good, but I am saying that, as God's family in Christ, we belong to one another and need one another in order to know God better and grow into "the whole measure of the fullness of Christ" (Eph. 4:13; cf. Rom. 12:5; 1 Cor. 12:12–27; Eph. 4:13–16).

Yet while each ethnic community possesses unique cultural treasure and wealth, each is also marred by cultural sin and impurity, according to Revelation 21:27. As John states unabashedly, "*Nothing impure will ever enter it* [the New Jerusalem], nor will anyone who does what is shameful or deceitful, but only those whose names are written in the Lamb's book of life" (emphasis added).

Every culture of which I am a part, and every nation on earth that has existed since the fall, has distinct cultural sins or "impurities." Just as sin infects us as individuals, it also perverts our larger ethnic cultures. These cultural impurities will not enter the New Jerusalem and the ultimate kingdom of our Father. This truth—that each culture contains distinct ethnic sin—is captured by Chicana feminist Gloria Anzaldúa: "Though I'll defend my race and culture when they are attacked by non-mexicanos, conosco el malestar de mi cultura. I abhor some of my culture's ways. . . . But I will not glorify those aspects of my culture which have injured me and which have injured me in the name of protecting me."[37]

And how do we distinguish between "glory and honor" and cultural sin? That is why Scripture is paramount as our cultural sieve and plumb line. As Christ enters our lives, he sanctifies us—both personally and culturally—based on the truth of God's Word (John 17:17).

To bring this conversation out of the abstract, I'll use my own Mexican and Latino cultures as an example. To be sure, Latino culture is diverse and complex, and yet, as exemplified in the lavish giving of Latino people, God is very generous and gracious and sometimes gives us more than we could hope for or imagine (Eph. 1:7–8; 3:20). No eye has seen, and no ear has heard, what God has prepared for those who love him and are called according to his purpose (1 Cor. 2:9). As

37. Anzaldúa, *Borderlands/La Frontera*, 21.

Latinos, we also share a precious family bond, which, at its best, reflects the unity of the body of Christ, also at its best. In keeping with Revelation 21:27, however, machismo and patriarchy stain Latino culture and fracture many of our families.

The five-hundred-year tradition of "Brown Theology"[38]— Latin American and US Latino social justice biblical reflection—is illustrative of the truth that, by God's design, every ethnic group brings a distinct perspective about the world, sacred Scripture, and who God is. I offer the Latino theology principle of "Galilee" as an example.

Latino and Latina theologians such as Virgilio Elizondo, Orlando Costas, and Elizabeth Conde-Frazier have reflected on the frequent mention of Galilee in the Gospels.[39] When God came in human flesh to bring salvation to the world, he chose to be raised in Galilee, do most of his ministry in Galilee, select his earliest leaders from Galilee, and, even after his resurrection, tell his followers to meet him in Galilee. Elizondo, Costas, and Conde-Frazier tell us that Galilee was the "hood" of Jesus's day. Galilee, and especially Nazareth of Galilee, was despised and rejected. Whereas Jerusalem was the center of socioeconomic, religious, and political life for the Jewish community, Galilee was a borderlands region that was shunned as a home to the culturally un-couth and mixed-race "mestizos." Because they were bilin-gual (speaking Aramaic and some Greek), Galileans spoke with an accent and were easily distinguishable once they opened their mouths. To make matters worse, they were not only looked down upon by their compatriots but also

38. Romero, *Brown Church*, 11.
39. Romero, *Brown Church*, 183–85. See, for example, Elizondo, *Galilean Journey*, 50–53; Costas, *Christ Outside the Gate*, 6; Martell-Otero, Maldonado Pérez, and Conde-Frazier, *Latina Evangélicas*, 112–13.

lived under the tyranny of Roman imperialism. Most were poor farmers, and many had lost their lands and money because of the excessive weight of Roman tribute, together with temple taxes. Drawing from an understanding of this historical context and decades of pastoral experience in the Latina/o community of San Antonio, Elizondo tells us that all of this reflects an important theological principle: "What human beings reject, God chooses as his very own."[40]

The famous musical *Hamilton* is also instructive of these biblical principles of the "glory and honor of the nations," as well as the cultural impurities that each of our cultures possesses because of the present reality of sin. Through creative and inspiring Broadway musical performance, *Hamilton* depicts the "glory and honor" of the founding of the United States. But it also shows how this glory and honor was tainted by the stain of racism toward African Americans.

My cross-cultural marriage has also given me the opportunity to witness Revelation 21:26–27 at work. With respect to "glory," I learn from my German midwestern in-laws about the values of industry and frugality (Prov. 6:6–11). I also learn about discipline in personal relationship with God (1 Cor. 8:24–27) and the importance of individual relationship with him (Rev. 3:20). With due respect, I have also observed that these values can sometimes go awry in midwestern culture when they get taken to the extreme. For example, a strong individuality and work ethic can make some blind to systemic and structural causes of poverty and cause them to overlook the many verses of Scripture that call us to compassion for immigrants and the poor.

40. Elizondo, *Galilean Journey*, 91.

## Racism Is Ordinary: From Glory and Honor to Racism in US History

Unfortunately, the diverse glory and honor or community cultural wealth of ethnic minorities in the United States has often gone unrecognized by majority white society. On an interpersonal level, this has often expressed itself as prejudice. Using the theological language we just described, prejudice says, "*My* glory and honor are better than yours, and I and my ethnic group reflect the image of God more than you and your people do. Your people have very little or no glory and honor compared to mine. Your people have lots of sin, but mine have no or very little sin."

In the language of Yosso and Chicano education scholars, as we discussed above, people of color in the United States are often portrayed through a cultural deficit lens. Politicians are among the most persistent purveyors of culturally deficient portrayals of ethnic communities in the United States, and as Nancy Yuen has shown, Hollywood finishes a close second.[41]

Racism transforms such ethnic prejudice into laws, policies, and social structures. Racism says, "Because my people have more glory and honor than yours do, I will create laws and policies so that my people gain more socioeconomic and political privilege than you and others from your ethnic community. This is only fair and right because you are inferior to me." An obvious example is seen in the laws of residential and educational segregation in the United States, which were not officially overturned until the 1960s.

Racism also creates social and legal categories to differentiate and divvy out privilege. Numerous CRT legal scholars, such as Ian Haney López (my former law school professor

41. Yuen, *Reel Inequality*, 6.

at Berkeley), have proven that from 1776 until the passage of the Civil Rights Act of 1964, the United States was officially structured around the social and legal category of "white."[42] "White" was not simply a neutral term of ethnic identification, such as "Scandinavian" or "French." It was an official legal category that bestowed on its possessor special rights of socioeconomic, political, and religious privilege. According to Delgado and Stefancic, such racialized categories are socially constructed and are products of social thought and relations. "They are not objective, inherent or fixed, [and] they correspond to no biological or genetic reality; rather, races are categories that society invents, manipulates, or retires, when convenient."[43] Dominant society racializes different ethnic groups in different ways in different times, in response to shifting circumstances of politics, economy, labor, and war.

As mentioned in the introduction, such prejudice and racism are "ordinary," according to CRT scholars. Though racism is always jarring, as people of color in the United States, we are not surprised when we experience racism because it is part of our common collective experience. We experience it on an institutional level too—in our schools, hospitals, courtrooms, political institutions, and unfortunately, even in some of our churches. According to CRT scholars, "Racism is ordinary, not aberrational—'normal science,' the usual way society does business, the common, everyday experience of most people of color in this country."[44] As discussed in the introduction, this idea of the ordinariness of racism squares clearly with the biblical notion that sin itself is ordinary.

The ordinariness of racism should not surprise us because it is borne out in multitudinous examples from time

---

42. Haney López, *White by Law*.
43. Delgado and Stefancic, *Critical Race Theory*, 13.
44. Delgado and Stefancic, *Critical Race Theory*, 7.

immemorial. Though racism in the modern sense of whites as superior to all other ethnic groups emerged out of the various racial projects of European and Euro-American colonization over the past five hundred years, the practice of creating legal categories to distinguish those of one ethnic group over another for purposes of divvying out socioeconomic and political privileges is as old as sin itself. Biblical examples include the enslavement of the Israelites in Egypt, as well as the case studies of the Babylonian, Persian, Greek, and Roman Empires, which all aimed for the military, economic, and cultural conquest of the Jewish people. Other illustrations include the tedious ancient Greek philosophical ruminations over the cultural category of "barbarian," China's contemporary tyrannical policies of persecution toward ethnic and religious minorities, and Mexico's five-century mistreatment of those labeled "Indian." We could spend ten volumes describing examples from across the world and across time, and we would just begin to scratch the surface. The social and legal classification of ethnic groups to create privilege for some and the disempowerment of others is a deeply embedded practice springing out reflexively from sinful human nature. Contrary to loud public clamors, especially among many white Christians, the United States is no exception.

CRT scholars within various fields, such as history, law, education, public health, and social work, have developed helpful analytical and theoretical tools to assist us in understanding the ways in which racism has played itself out in US society. As previously mentioned, for example, Haney López has traced the legal history of the concept of whiteness in the US legal system. He and many others have proven that until the Civil Rights Acts of 1964, the social and legal category of "white" was an official structure of the United

States. In fact, between 1790 and 1952, naturalization as a US citizen was limited to those legally defined as white. The institution of marriage was also impacted by such racial bias. The Expatriation Act of 1907 stripped white women of their US citizenship as a consequence of marriage to immigrant husbands. On a state level, anti-miscegenation laws were common and not banned on a national level until the Supreme Court case of *Loving v. Virginia* in 1967.

The stakes were high. If you were considered "white by law," then you and your family received all the best socioeconomic and political benefits the United States had to offer. You could live where you wanted or be hired in any job. Your kids could go to the best schools and universities or swim in the local pool any day of the week (except for the day reserved for blacks and Latinos). You would not be turned away from your local hospital, could eat at any restaurant in town, and could sit in any movie theater seat or church pew. If you were not considered "white," well, then you didn't have access to any of these things. "White" was a treasured legal and racial status because it came along with preferential treatment and privilege in every arena of society. To use the language of African American sociologist George Lipsitz, whiteness had a "cash value."[45] This is how "race" was created in America.

Except for those of northern and western European stock, the legal definition of who was white was a shifting target fought about in the courts. Anyone who wasn't white struggled for inclusion in the whiteness club. As part of what became known as the "racial prerequisite" cases, from 1878 to 1952, US courts became the arbiters of "whiteness."[46] Courts

45. Lipsitz, *Possessive Investment in Whiteness*, vii.
46. Haney López, *White by Law*, 1–2.

embraced two major approaches that were based on "common knowledge" and "scientific evidence" and evaluated factors such as skin color, facial features, national origin, language, and culture.[47] Immigrants of Chinese, Japanese, Italian, Armenian, Mexican, Syrian, Arabian, South Asian, and Filipino descent all went to court to establish their whiteness. Italians, Armenians, and Mexicans "won" their battles for legal whiteness; the others did not.

As LatCrit and AsianCrit scholars such as Laura Gómez and Bill Ong Hing have documented for decades, US immigration history over the past 150 years has been shaped around whiteness and the exclusion of those deemed less racially desirable.[48] Anti-Chinese xenophobia produced invidious legislation, such as the Chinese Exclusion Act of 1882, which for the first time in US history barred an entire ethnic group from immigration. Racism toward Italians and Eastern Europeans fueled the passage of the Emergency Quota Act of 1921, the Cable Act of 1922, and the Immigration Act of 1924. Together with the Tydings-McDuffie Act (1934), these laws slowed immigration from Asia and southern and eastern Europe to a trickle and expanded migration flows from northern and western Europe. Between 1930 and 1935, repatriations and deportations of Mexicans totaled 345,839. Tragically, Mexican Americans were also not excluded from these deportations. In California, over 80 percent of the repatriates were citizens or legal residents of the United States. Moreover, between 1947 and 1954 the Immigration and Nationalization Service boasted of apprehending more than one million unauthorized Mexican immigrants as part of the notorious Operation Wetback. Racially discriminatory

47. Haney López, *White by Law*, 3.
48. Gómez, *Manifest Destinies*, 140; Hing, *Making and Remaking Asian America*, 17–42.

quotas favoring northern and western European immigrants and barring immigrants from Asia, Latin America, Africa, and southern and eastern Europe were not overturned until the passage of the Immigration and Nationality Act of 1965.[49]

In addition to being a legal category, whiteness was also a dominant social identity. Not only did it give its beneficiaries privileged access to racialized social structures and systems, but it also transferred a powerful psychological sense of racial superiority. Those who were accepted as white felt themselves superior to those who were not and therefore clung to the social identity of whiteness. They were the "real" Americans. All others were culturally, biologically, and even religiously inferior. CRT scholars refer to this as the "psychic" benefits of white social identity. This in part explains why some poor whites express some of the most racist attitudes toward immigrants and other ethnic minorities and have recently gravitated toward the Make America Great Again movement. Their sense of racial superiority bolsters their sense of self-esteem even though they themselves are "Galileans."

Redlining maps of the 1930s provide a vivid description of historical racial attitudes, which have since made a resurgence, in particular during the presidency of Donald Trump. As a result of the racial logic of Manifest Destiny, which stated that Anglo-Saxon Protestants were superior to all other ethnic and religious groups, combined with the official sanction of restrictive covenants, the United States, until 1965, was legally carved up into "Goshens"—explicitly segregated communities of Latinos, Asians, African Americans, and even Poles, Italians, and Jews. Then, as now, the United States lent money to banks, which in turn gave mortgages

49. Romero, "Migration as Grace," 18–19.

to prospective home buyers. The federal government created underwriting policies that barred banks from lending to individuals who wished to purchase in areas that were designated red—which is where the term *redlined* comes from. The following map is of segregated Los Angeles in 1938. The red areas were segregated communities where people of color lived. The green areas were racially exclusive, reserved for rich whites. The yellow areas were one step below red, and the blue areas were one step below green.[50]

A realtor's description of the redlined community of Boyle Heights in 1939 (where I was born, and where my father's family lived for many years) paints a stark picture of the reality of the segregation and racist vitriol of the time. All but white Anglo-Saxon Protestants were shunned and were the subject of xenophobic ire: "Russian, Polish & Armenian Jews, Slavs, Greeks, American Mexicans, Japanese and Italians. . . . Subversive racial elements increasing. . . . This is a 'melting pot' area and is literally honeycombed with diverse and subversive racial elements. It is seriously doubted whether there is a single block in the area which does not contain detrimental racial elements."[51]

Realtors of Pasadena during this era expressed similar racial concerns about Northwest Pasadena. In this case, Mexicans and blacks were the disparaged racial and cultural groups: "Both Mexican and Negro population increasing. . . . This old unrestricted area has long been inhabited by the servant class who were employed by wealthy families in the

50. Richard Marciano, Chien-Yi Hou, and David Goldberg, "Color Codes," T-RACES: Testbed for the Redlining Archives of California's Exclusionary Spaces, accessed July 30, 2022, http://t-races.net/T-RACES/colormap.html.

51. Richard Marciano, Chien-Yi Hou, and David Goldberg, "Boyle Heights Description File, 1939," T-RACES: Testbed for the Redlining Archives of California's Exclusionary Spaces, accessed July 30, 2022, http://t-races.net/T-RACES/data/la/ad/ad0417.pdf.

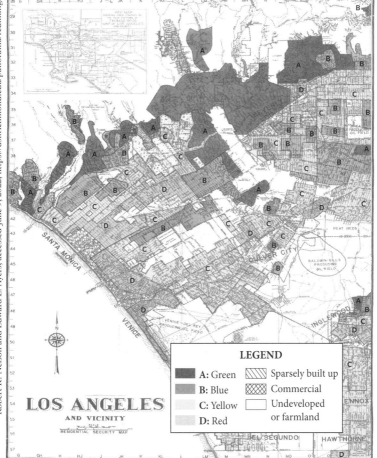

Public Domain / Courtesy of Robert K. Nelson et al., "Mapping Inequality," in American Panorama, ed. Robert K. Nelson and Edward L. Ayers, accessed June 9, 2022, https://dsl.richmond.edu/panorama/redlining.

Figure 1.1 Map of Segregated Los Angeles.

higher grade areas to the west and south. This district was originally much smaller but constant infiltration into other sections as deed restrictions expired has created a real menace which is greatly concerning property owners of Pasadena and Altadena."[52]

52. Richard Marciano, Chien-Yi Hou, and David Goldberg, "Pasadena Description File, 1939," T-RACES: Testbed for the Redlining Archives of California's

During this era, Anglo elites preserved their hubs of racial privilege through the use of racially restrictive covenants. Such covenants were legally enforceable in a court of law and essentially stated that the homeowner promised never to sell their house to a non-white person. As reflected in the following realtor description of Arcadia, California, such segregation was expected to be permanent, to last "in perpetuity":

Foreign Families: 0%
Negro: 0%
Shifting or Infiltration: None apparent

. . . Deed restrictions provide for single family structures with a minimum of 2500 sq. ft. to be constructed under architectural supervision. *Racial protection is in perpetuity.* Conveniences, including recreational facilities, are all as available as is desirable for an area of this character.[53]

Segregated housing in turn gave rise to segregated parks, pools, schools, hospitals, restaurants, movie theaters, hiking trails, mortuaries—and even churches. Stated another way, segregated housing gave birth to inequitable socioeconomic, legal, and political structures. The green areas had the best housing, schools, parks, hospitals, legal services, and so forth; the red areas did not. In this way, the systems and structures of US society became racialized. This is what we refer to as "systemic" sin. This racialized legacy in the United States continues even in the present moment.

Exclusionary Spaces, accessed July 30, 2022, http://t-races.net/T-RACES/data/la/ad/ad0370.pdf.

53. Richard Marciano, Chien-Yi Hou, and David Goldberg, "Santa Anita Area Description File, 1939," T-RACES: Testbed for the Redlining Archives of California's Exclusionary Spaces, accessed July 30, 2022, http://t-races.net/T-RACES/data/la/ad/ad0027.pdf (emphasis added).

Today, most of the green areas are still green, and most of the red areas are still red. Some of the areas that were once blue and yellow have now become red because of white flight, and some of the areas that, until recently, were red are now becoming green because of gentrification. The constant is that we brown and black folks continue to occupy the red Goshens of our time. In Southern California, for example, cities such as San Marino, Newport Beach, Pacific Palisades, and Beverly Hills still possess the best housing, schools, parks, hospitals, and legal services; on the other hand, neighborhoods such as East Los Angeles, South Los Angeles, Northwest Pasadena, and Santa Ana are largely characterized by underfunded schools, inadequate housing, fewer parks, and lack of access to quality health care and legal services.

Mountains of data bear out the continued persistence of structural and systemic inequality along the lines of race in the United States. This reality is borne out across categories of poverty, hunger, health care, education, and mass incarceration. For example, in 2019, the median black household earned only sixty-one cents for every dollar of income earned by the median white household; the median Hispanic household earned seventy-four cents in comparison. Largely as a consequence of historical residential segregation and redlining, white families possess more wealth than black and Hispanic families, several times over. In 2019, one-quarter of African American children and one in five Latino children lived in poverty. No child of any ethnic background should ever have to experience poverty, and African American children were three times as likely as white children to face circumstances of poverty.[54] As a natural

54. Valerie Wilson, "Racial Disparities in Income and Poverty Remain Largely Unchanged amid Strong Income Growth in 2019," *Working Economics Blog*,

outgrowth of economic hardship, food insecurity is also stratified along racial lines, with 22 percent of black households and 18 percent of Latino households experiencing hunger.[55]

With respect to health care, 39 percent of Latino immigrants and 25 percent of all Latinos have no health insurance.[56] Even among ethnic minorities who have health care, the treatment they receive is documented to be of lower quality than that of whites with the same level of health care. A report by the National Academy of Medicine (NAM) found that "racial and ethnic minorities receive lower-quality health care than white people—even when insurance status, income, age, and severity of conditions are comparable." Ethnic minorities are less likely than white people to be provided advanced treatments for stroke and cancer and less likely to receive services such as kidney dialysis or transplants. According to NAM, "Some people in the United States were more likely to die from cancer, heart disease, and diabetes simply because of their race or ethnicity, not just because they lack access to health care."[57]

Though most schools in the United States were officially desegregated between 1954 and 1970, African American chil-

Economic Policy Institute, September 16, 2020, https://www.epi.org/blog/racial-disparities-in-income-and-poverty-remain-largely-unchanged-amid-strong-income-growth-in-2019/.

55. Greg Kaufmann, "Want to Eradicate Hunger in America? Take on Racism," *Nation*, February 4, 2019, https://www.thenation.com/article/archive/hunger-food-insecurity-racism-mariana-chilton/.

56. Jens Manuel Krogstad and Mark Hugo Lopez, "Hispanic Immigrants More Likely to Lack Health Insurance than U.S.-Born," Pew Research Center, September 26, 2014, http://www.pewresearch.org/fact-tank/2014/09/26/higher-share-of-hispanic-immigrants-than-u-s-born-lack-health-insurance/.

57. Quoted in Khiara M. Bridges, "Implicit Bias and Racial Disparities in Health Care," *Human Rights Magazine*, November 19, 2018, https://www.american bar.org/groups/crsj/publications/human_rights_magazine_home/the-state-of-healthcare-in-the-united-states/racial-disparities-in-health-care/.

dren are still five times more likely than white children to attend schools that are highly segregated by race and ethnicity. They are also more than twice as likely to attend high-poverty schools than their white peers.[58] School segregation for Latino students is actually worse today than it was for the previous generation. Latino students in the ten poorest school districts in the country attend schools that have, on average, only 5 percent white students.[59]

Beyond education and health care, Latino and African American men are also overrepresented in our nation's prisons and are incarcerated at a rate much higher than their white counterparts. Among black men in their early thirties, for example, 8 percent are imprisoned as compared to 1.2 percent of white men of the same age.[60] In 2015, approximately 9.1 percent of young black men and 3 percent of young Hispanic men were incarcerated on any given day, as opposed to 1.6 percent of white men.[61]

As Latinos and African Americans, we are the Galileans of today. In the words of noted African American theologian Howard Thurman, we are those "standing with our backs against the wall."[62] And yet, drawing from our faith in Jesus and our resources of centuries of God-given spiritual capital and community cultural wealth, we persevere. We struggle. We persist.

58. Emma García, "Schools Are Still Segregated, and Black Children Are Paying a Price," Economic Policy Institute, February 12, 2020, https://www .epi.org/publication/schools-are-still-segregated-and-black-children-are-paying -a-price/.
59. Fuller et al., "Worsening School Segregation."
60. William J. Sabol, Heather Couture, and Paige M. Harrison, "Prisoners in 2006," Bureau of Justice Statistics Bulletin, U.S. Department of Justice, December 2007, https://bjs.ojp.gov/content/pub/pdf/p06.pdf; Christian and Thomas, "Examining the Intersections," 69.
61. Pettit and Gutierrez, "Mass Incarceration and Racial Inequality," 1159.
62. Thurman, *Jesus and the Disinherited*, 7.

## Conclusion: Called from a Future Hope

John's vision of the beloved community from every nation, tribe, people, and language is the future to which we are called. In the words of Justo González, "This is the vision from which, out of which, the church must live. The church lives not only out of its past, but also out of its future; not only out of its efficient cause, but also out of its final cause."[63] We are called from a future hope.[64] If only we have eyes to see, the book of Revelation is God's heavenly vision for the multicultural kingdom of God.

John makes it clear, however, that the fulfillment of this multicultural eschatological goal requires effort and healing. For indeed, even after Eden is restored, "the leaves of the tree are for the healing of the nations" (Rev. 22:2), and though the glory and honor of the nations will be brought into the New Jerusalem, "nothing impure will ever enter it, nor will anyone who does what is shameful or deceitful, but only those whose names are written in the Lamb's book of life" (Rev. 21:26–27).

As people of color in the United States, we long for that day. Like Jesus, our savior from Galilee, we bear many wounds. We long for the church in America to live into this future healing now. We long for the church to clearly acknowledge the racial deceit that shaped the impure history of colonialism, slavery, and segregation in this country and to repent of the racialized attitudes, systems, and structures that continue to harm us now. A distorted American exceptionalism that seeks to claim the glory and honor of the United States while ignoring its historic cultural sins is unbiblical because it implies, falsely, that Revelation 21:26–27 applies

---

63. González, *For the Healing of the Nations*, 103–4.
64. González, *For the Healing of the Nations*, 99.

to all nations except itself. Such arrogant cultural pride will only perpetuate ethnic division.

The theology of the glory and honor of the nations might seem romantic to some, and abstract and overstated to others, but the stakes of this biblical understanding are especially high for the US church. Every year 1.2 million young people are leaving the US church—one every twenty-six seconds. Many are leaving because they do not feel that their God-given glory and honor is welcome. In a similar way, many pastors and ministry leaders are abandoning their denominations and institutions because their God-given cultural lenses and perspectives have been disregarded, and they are not being promoted into positions of significant organizational authority. They feel that they do not belong because they are asked, intentionally or unintentionally, to leave their God-given glory and honor outside the ministry door.

What would it look like to reimagine our churches and ministries in a way that honors and integrates the community cultural wealth of the diverse peoples of the body of Christ? What will it take to reframe our churches and ministries in a way that centers the God-given cultural wisdom and perspectives of our brothers and sisters in Christ who come from backgrounds that are different from our own? It is to these complex questions, and an application of Revelation 21:26–27, that we will turn in chapter 3. Before we turn to those questions of institutional reconstruction, however, we must examine our individualistic doctrines of sin that often get in the way.

# 2

# Fall

## Sin and Racism—the Ordinary Businesses of Society

### Introduction

"It's 2020! I can't believe this is still happening." In 2020, when anti-Asian racism surged in the United States during the global COVID-19 pandemic, I (Jeff) received numerous messages and texts communicating this well-intended shock. Friends and colleagues called to express their regret that this kind of bigotry "still" takes place. While I generally receive these friendly messages with gratitude, I am sadly aware that surprise and shock are manifestations of a mythical view of a polite society in which racial discrimination and bigotry are rare (though, they are coming to be viewed as less rare in these troubling days) and are attributable to a tiny sliver of the fringe, antisocial, radically impolite.[1] However, not all respond with this minimal, new credulity. Clergy colleagues and congregation members have responded to reports of racial incidents with total disbelief and denial. "It *can't* be that bad," they say. Both shock and disbelief express a mythical view, one in which racism is an aberration.

For many persons and communities of color (though certainly not all), experiences of racism are unsurprising. Critical race theorists, as discussed above, say that these experiences are "ordinary."[2] W. E. B. Du Bois gestures toward the ordinariness of racism in his own experience when, after writing wistfully of emancipation, he reckons with the ongoing reality of racial injustice:

> Years have passed away since then—ten, twenty, forty; forty years of national life, forty years of renewal and development, and yet the swarthy spectre sits in its accustomed seat at the Nation's feast. In vain do we cry to this our vastest social problem:
>
> > "Take any shape but that, and my firm nerves
> > Shall never tremble!"
>
> The Nation has not yet found peace from its sins; the freedman has not yet found in freedom his promised land.[3]

1. It is also troubling when racist misconduct is attributed to "crazy" people. This attribution is problematic in several ways. First, as I will argue below, critical race theorists have identified the way in which racism is far from irrational and is instead a form of contemporary "common sense" (see n. 18). Second, this response is sometimes little more than an attempt to distance oneself from the most impolite forms of racism while one is still highly invested in systems of injustice. Third, such a colloquialism unmasks forms of ableism that keep people of all abilities from meaningful and mutual experiences of community.

2. Delgado and Stefancic, *Critical Race Theory*.

3. Du Bois, *Souls of Black Folk*, 7.

The freedom that emancipation won was not itself adequate. Du Bois goes on to analyze the ways that would-be markers of progress, such as voting rights in the Fifteenth Amendment and access to education, did not yield liberty. Seven decades after the 1903 publication of *The Souls of Black Folk*, the United States continued to retrace the razor wire of Du Bois's "color line," which he experienced as the qualitative difference in experience and relationship across racial difference. In 1973, American evangelical leaders signed the Chicago Declaration of Evangelical Social Concern. This group of leaders confessed and acknowledged the seriousness of racial injustice and economic exploitation. One passage reads, "We deplore the historic involvement of the church in America with racism and the conspicuous responsibility of the evangelical community for perpetuating the personal attitudes and institutional structures that have divided the body of Christ along color lines." Among the signatories were white evangelical leaders and scholars like Carl F. H. Henry, Richard Mouw, and Bernard Ramm. There were also leaders and scholars of color like Samuel Escobar, John Perkins, and William Pannell. The Chicago Declaration would be renewed two decades later, in 1993, as a new set of signatories would "weep over the persistence of racism."[4]

In this chapter we contend that the raucous public discord in which CRT is repeatedly (and often speciously) named is emblematic of an uninterrupted legacy of callousness to the voices and cries of people and communities of color that suffer white supremacy. There is a sense in which Jim Wallis's aphorism that racism is "America's original sin" is applicable to a framing of this legacy.[5] As critical race theorists

4. "The 1993 Chicago Declaration," Center for Public Justice, 2022, https://www.cpjustice.org/public/page/content/chicago_declaration.

5. Wallis, *America's Original Sin*.

have shown through their critique of the legal principles and documents that birthed the United States, the juridical and ideological machinery that reproduce racial injustice have been in place from the beginning. Furthermore, our analysis in this chapter will consider various Christian traditions' formulations of the doctrine of sin, examining the unspoken commitments that lead Christians to react instinctively and negatively against CRT. Finally, we will look at the ways an individual, a ministry team, a church, or organization engages racial injustice and how this engagement turns, to some extent, on an understanding of the craftiness, cunning, innovation, and devastations of racism in the modern day—the very subject matter on which CRT is perhaps most articulate.

The statement "Racism is ordinary" may be one of the most threatening claims that can be made about life in the United States. If this were an innocuous claim, pundits would not go to such lengths to reframe it for their audiences as a threat to precious American institutions. For example, the Heritage Foundation, a conservative think tank in Washington, DC, encourages its audience members to become "whistleblowers" when they perceive the use of CRT in their children's schools, in the workplace, and in the military.[6] The think tank propounds its antagonistic perspective of CRT so that those in its audience do not have to read primary sources for themselves. In so doing, it criticizes works, like Robin DiAngelo's *White Fragility*, which are *not* works of CRT. What we have here, then, is the deliberate ideological misuse of the term *critical race theory* for a culture war in which there is little by way of either faithful or constructive

---

6. "Critical Race Theory: Facts, Issues, and Solutions," Heritage Foundation, accessed April 29, 2022, https://www.heritage.org/critical-race-theory.

engagement and in which there will be no winners.[7] We can all do better by pursuing honest and accurate consideration of CRT's claims.

Why do critical race theorists make this claim about the ordinariness of racism, and what exactly is meant by it? Honest consideration requires that we address the meaning of the word *racism*. Two camps are clearly divided over the sense of this word. On the one hand, there are those for whom racism can only ever be personal hatred toward an individual of another race. In this view, racism exists in one's attitudes, is illogical, can manifest in outward acts of violence, and is seen as a historical artifact that the United States has mostly moved past. On the other hand, there are those who understand that racism is not limited to one's attitudes. They view racism as being related to outcomes, systems, and structures as much as, if not more than, to the individual actors who uphold, participate in, and benefit from these systems.

This is where the ideological divide persists. Even the phrase "systems and structures" has become a trigger for skeptics who *mis*understand it as code for CRT, which they have already concluded they should reject. Because of this misunderstanding, using these words may not be beneficial *if* the goal is to remain in constructive engagement with skeptics of CRT. There are, however, examples of systems and structures that broad swaths of the American public can easily identify, and we will explore these in a moment. First, however, a Christian engagement with CRT, aimed at seeing and understanding *together*, benefits from shared theological

---

7. See, for example, conservative activist Christopher Rufo (@realchrisrufo), "We have successfully," Twitter, March 15, 2021, 3:14 p.m., https://twitter.com /realchrisrufo/status/1371540368714428416.

language (even if there is some variation of conviction by theological tradition).

## Sin as Ordinary

I (Jeff) recall walking through the center of the University of Michigan one cool morning and meeting one of the varieties of open-air "fire and brimstone" preachers who came to campus on a periodic basis. I would eventually learn to respect the ways these preachers sometimes (though certainly not always) exercised civility and compassion before hostile audiences. What always irked my sensibilities, however, was their insistence on making condemnation their first move with students as they passed by. They would enumerate the sins that, in their rhetorical approach, were sending the students at whom they pointed "straight to hell." Naturally, this raised the ire of the students, which led me to wonder why these preachers would choose such an approach. So one day I decided I should ask!

On the occasion in question, I asked an older Asian American man why he did not take the log out of his own eye before he accused others of sin. This would become my first real encounter with a regretfully uninformed and narrow version of the Wesleyan doctrine of Christian perfection— a belief that Charles Wesley expounded during the First Great Awakening. This view (which, on this side of heaven, I do not share) draws the hope of blamelessness in this life from 1 Thessalonians 5:23. I can understand why that hope, combined with the view that sin is voluntary and within one's control, might lead to the view that the Christian life includes the possibility of grace-fueled progress in thought, word, and deed, which would make "perfection" achievable.

"Well, do you read your Bible every day?" he asked. I was shocked that he chose inconsistent Bible reading as the moral failing that would keep me from inclusion in God's family. He would dismiss my youthful zeal as I argued inarticulately for the centrality of grace and forgiveness in Christ. The effects of that encounter lasted for months. My personal responsibility for sin came into sharp focus as I pondered the vicissitudes of the journey toward sanctification. Perhaps more importantly, I began to reflect soteriologically on Jesus's final words in John 19:30: "It is finished." What could that mean? What was finished? How so?

It was around this time that I read J. I. Packer's essay "What Did the Cross Achieve?" In it, Packer advances the penal substitution view of the atonement. He argues that in contrast to two other important views of the atonement (i.e., the moral influence, or moral exemplar, theory and *Christus Victor*), penal substitution "grounds man's plight as a victim of sin and Satan in the fact that, for all God's daily goodness to him, as a sinner he stands under divine judgment."[8] Packer treads judiciously: that Christ is our *substitute* and that his death was the *penalty* for our sins does not deny that Jesus's death was morally exemplary, nor that it is effective in freeing us from principalities and powers that oppress God's beloved. In fact, in all three views that Packer treats, sin is in various senses ordinary, and the cross of Christ is God's gracious answer.[9]

8. Packer, "What Did the Cross Achieve?," 20.

9. I will note that many are coming to regret that the Bible teaches penal substitution (and to question whether it does), or that so many Christians allow their ethics to work out of an exclusively penal substitutionary framework. Among the undergrad and grad students with whom I've worked since 2001, there is a growing concern that the evangelical church considers divine violence as justification for its own toleration of many forms of violence (from racism and sexism to retributive approaches in criminal justice). Additionally, the conversation around atonement in the theological academy—even in evangelical circles—has shifted quite a bit

While I can appreciate Packer's essay, my own sense has been that the challenge racism presents to our understanding of culpability has exceeded the capacity of increasingly narrow, popular formulations of the doctrines of sin and atonement. To illustrate the need to draw on the whole range of the Bible's vocabulary for our human condition, Cornelius Plantinga has created a fictional account of a white racist, Jim Bob, who learned racism at an early age from his family of origin: "What Jim Bob's racism shows us is that moral evil is social and structural as well as personal: it comprises a vast historical and cultural matrix that includes traditions, old patterns of relationship and behavior, atmospheres of expectation, social habits. Of course, culpability in social and structural evil is notoriously hard to assess."[10]

Plantinga carves out a definition of sin as "culpable shalom-breaking." It is easy enough for him to describe the impressive scope of shalom-breaking, but it becomes important for him to take time and care to defend culpability. Individual accountability, or culpability, is a key component of this definition of sin. The thoroughness of Plantinga's account, however, is not in his definition of the word *sin* but in the many words he explores to describe the Scripture's teaching. Sin is not just individual culpable acts but "corruption," "perversion," "pollution," "disintegration," "folly," and more.

Nevertheless, the narrow focus on culpability in so much white evangelical hamartiology excludes the other senses of our fallenness that we get from the Scripture. As I survey various traditions' confessions, statements of faith, and doctrinal positions, I've begun to suspect that the way Christians

to include other views besides penal substitution. See, for example, Beilby and Eddy, *Nature of the Atonement.*

10. Plantinga, *Not the Way It's Supposed to Be,* 25.

understand the scope and nature of sin can be mapped onto one's posture toward CRT. Those who consider racism to be constrained to an individual's attitudes and actions have likely been shaped by, or may resonate more strongly with, an understanding of sin that foregrounds an individual's attitudes.

This is not news. After all, there is no escaping the interiority of the word *heart* in the Bible. Some Christians in cross-racial interactions are concerned that their good intentions are overlooked. So they appeal to their "heart" when the impact of their actions is "unintentionally" hurtful. And yes, we know that God has the ability to do this: "the Lord looks at the heart," in distinction to, among other things, outward appearance (1 Sam. 16:7). In other words, the liberal individualists' focus on—and proof-texted justification for—private spirituality, personal morality, and free will should be expected as byproducts of the cultural waters in which Western Christians swim.

At this point in the development of this discourse in the United States, I believe that we can forgo retracing the contours of the "accountable freewill individualism" that Michael Emerson and Christian Smith offered twenty years ago.[11] I say this because I believe that Christian theology in the West has committed to a turn away from individualism. To be clear, I do not see that our habits have changed significantly but rather that the language intended to cultivate a new social imaginary has changed. I see more seminarians and preachers writing and talking about the importance of cultivating community. So far, whatever they mean by *community* seems dangerously thin. Furthermore, I have yet to see serious learning from or submission to Christian

---

11. Emerson and Smith, *Divided by Faith*, 76–79.

communities in which the communal imagination has been thickly formative for generations. Nevertheless, I suspect that the days of dogmatically individualistic biblical interpretation and theology are numbered—even if this change is merely a part of the long, moral arc of the universe instead of the result of a single, disruptive intervention or crisis moment.

Therefore, sin as individual, culpable, moral failure in action and in attitude will have to share space with other biblical formulations to form a more comprehensive account of the Scripture's teaching. God does not *only* look at the heart. Most directly for this discussion, God sees the absurdity of Pharoah's gall to impugn the Israelites as lazy when it was Pharoah's elaborate cruelty that built an empire of horrors upon a slave economy (Exod. 5:8). God sees Israel's ruling class tragically parroting Egypt's idolatry as they oppress their own people by using counterfeit weights and measures in commerce and by setting agricultural policies that rob the poor of staple foods (see Amos 8:4–6). In Jesus's day, God sees the area of the temple that is set aside for gentile worship being turned into a "den of robbers" in which both the glory of God and God-fearing gentiles have been robbed of their due.[12]

These examples of "systemic and structural sin" are, frankly, low-hanging fruit. Those who deliberately misconstrue these as *only* individual, moral failings might not be persuaded by a chapter like this. However, there are many others of sincere biblical conviction and good will who are open to remaining in communion and whose convictions leave them concerned about what seems so pedestrian to us.

---

12. Here in the Synoptic Gospels (Matt. 21:13; Mark 11:17; Luke 19:46), Jesus is quoting the words of Jer. 7:11.

For example, the president of the Southern Baptist Theological Seminary, Al Mohler, has repeatedly articulated his concern that systemic and structural sin, while real, should not be afforded priority over "individual culpability." Mohler acknowledges that "individual sins eventually take structural form. The structures then both facilitate and rationalize ongoing and expanding individual sin."[13]

If I understand them correctly, Mohler and others consider the "biblical gospel" to be focused on the glorious work of Christ on the cross to accomplish forgiveness for sins—where sins are understood as individual, culpable transgressions against a holy God. I think it would be charitable to read them as being concerned about due attention being diverted from Christ's love for individuals to the point that this emphasis is lost. In a positive sense, this would be an attempt to highlight the "antithetical" uniqueness of Christian theology vis-à-vis legal scholarship. That is, Christian theology offers its own account of the origins of and solutions to our individual and social problems that is, in many ways, antithetical to non-Christian accounts. Again, at its best, this theological account is not treated as mutually exclusive of the accounts from other disciplines.

For example, in June of 2019, Mohler's Southern Baptist Convention (SBC) passed a resolution titled "Critical Race Theory and Intersectionality" that reflected its concern about CRT.[14] In the resolution, the authors accurately observe that "evangelical scholars who affirm the authority and

13. Albert R. Mohler Jr., "Systemic Racism, God's Grace, and the Human Heart: What the Bible Teaches about Structural Sin," *Public Discourse: The Journal of the Witherspoon Institute*, June 25, 2020, https://www.thepublicdiscourse.com/2020/06/65536/.

14. To be clear, I am treating the SBC statement as broadly representative of convictions held, but often unspoken, by many white evangelical Christians, not just Southern Baptists.

sufficiency of Scripture have employed selective insights from critical race theory and intersectionality to understand multifaceted social dynamics" and that "these analytical tools can aid in evaluating a variety of human experiences." The authors reason that the doctrine of general revelation "accounts for truthful insights found in human ideas that do not explicitly emerge from Scripture and reflects what some may term 'common grace.'"[15] So far, these convictions leave ample space for Christians to make significant (if not full) use of CRT.

However, the authors of the resolution also make sure to articulate their priority for the "categories and principles" they see emerging from Scripture. As it pertains to the doctrine of sin, the SBC makes at least two principial moves. First, the authors aver that the "root cause" from which social problems emerge is "sin"—a theological concept that does *not* serve as a starting principle of a legal theory like CRT. In this short document, the authors do not explain what they think comprises CRT's account of the ordinariness of racism. Nevertheless, their suspicion becomes transparent in the resolution; namely, they are concerned that CRT is advancing a "transcendent ideological framework" that competes with their account of a sinful world. I believe that by doing so, the authors force themselves into a category mistake by assuming an oppositional relationship between their (and others') doctrine of sin and CRT's critical analysis of the legal system. Correcting the category mistake as it relates to the doctrine of sin is one of the goals of highlighting the continuity between this doctrine and CRT's treatment of racism.

15. "On Critical Race Theory and Intersectionality," Southern Baptist Convention, June 1, 2019, https://www.sbc.net/resource-library/resolutions/on-critical-race-theory-and-intersectionality/.

Second, the authors gesture toward their concern about the "categories" into which human beings are divided. They focus their theological anthropology on "unity in Christ amid image bearers." As a result, they are concerned about "categories identified as sinful in Scripture" that might compete with our image bearing, on the one hand, and other "divinely affirmed distinctions," on the other. It is not clearly expressed, but it seems that among these divinely affirmed distinctions, the authors believe that "ethnic, gender, and cultural distinctions exist and are a gift from God." Then, without naming them, they leave it to the reader to supply *racial* distinctions as those categories identified as sinful in Scripture.

Before we continue, I observe in this concern about racial categories a significant acknowledgment and awareness of systemic sin for which I commend the authors of the SBC statement. Racial categories are a serious theological problem. First, racial categories are widely acknowledged to be socially constructed. In fact, for quite disparate purposes, Christians across the ideological spectrum have made the same claim—namely, that because of its social construction, race ought not be granted ontological status. Toward one end, some seek to deny an emphasis on racial difference in favor of the reality of our shared humanity, toward which the people of God are journeying even now. On the other end of the spectrum, some seek to deconstruct the ways in which racial difference is treated as a primordial, anthropological fact, to the detriment of people of color.

Across this large swath of the spectrum, many agree that humans are not to be treated as if their racial categorization were somehow primordial in origin (the very mistake made by the racist "Curse of Ham" perspective used to justify the enslavement of what theologians reflecting on race sometimes call "dark flesh"—a term that highlights, among other things, the global nature of this phenomenon). This acknowledgment should not escape our attention. When Christians are aware that race and racialization are, in part, constructed in our imaginations as a result of historic abuses, racist systems, and unjust structures (e.g., the institution of chattel slavery, the Doctrine of Discovery, discriminatory sentencing laws), they demonstrate awareness of systemic sin. So to demur at or deny the importance and prevalence of systems and structures in the midst of this ideologically fraught conversation about CRT is a mistake. It seems to me a manner of forgetting the reality that has already been established in Scripture and that is readily observable in everyone's everyday lives: systems and structures are an undeniably influential part of our human experience and social world. To deliberately ignore them by turning inward to the "heart" (which, to be clear, not all Western Christians do) is a strange forgetting indeed.

Not all doctrinal systems, however, so readily enable believers to forget the systems and structures that pervade our lives. Anthony Thiselton has already provided a helpful, diachronic look at nonindividualist hamartiologies. Below, I provide a few derivative highlights that serve to widen the scope of the doctrine of sin beyond culpable failures of individual moral agents (which, to be clear, is a well-attested view that on the whole should not be rejected) and relate them to the present conversation about racism.[16]

- Thiselton writes that for Tertullian, vis-à-vis Scripture, "Sin is not merely an individual affair. A

16. The highlights that follow are drawn from Thiselton, *Systematic Theology*, chap. 7.

supposedly individual sin may actually affect families and social environments."[17] If racism, like sin, is transmissible through families and social environments, one might expect that it becomes the normalized state of affairs, invisibilized, and eventually defended as the status quo.

- Ambrose emphasizes the corporate fall of humanity in Adam instead of in isolated acts. We inherit a state of sinful*ness*. In pastoral practice, I have frequently been asked about whether an act is sinful. My reply is often to highlight the sinful condition we inhabit. To extend this further, it is common for Western Christians to fixate on instances or acts of racial prejudice or violence rather than on our thoroughly racialized conditions.

- Augustine of Hippo argues against Pelagius, citing Romans 5:12, and understands sin as both universal and individual. In my own thinking, it is the universality of sin that creates a sense of ordinariness. At the very least, to say that "racism is ordinary," as some critical race theorists do, is to say that it pervades society as "the way things are."

- Thomas Aquinas articulates a view of sin as the punishment for sin. In other words, sinning once can incline us to sin again, and more. The way naked expressions of white supremacy became an acceptable feature of political and social life in the United States—a kind of "common sense," if you will—is an example of this theological perspective.[18]

---

17. Thiselton, *Systematic Theology*, 156.

18. In this chapter, I will refer to "common sense" in two ways. Critical race theorists refer to a kind of common sense that makes racism invisible. That is, a policy or structure could not possibly be problematically racist if it makes good,

- John Calvin describes the total inability of human beings, apart from God, to pursue what is good. Only by the gracious move of God toward human beings in Christ can we be set free from our bondage to sin. It is troubling, then, when Christians presume that their relationships with others across race are unimpeachable, their intentions pure and unquestionable.

- Karl Barth's theological formulation regarding sin strikes at the heart of the matter. Sin is pride that expresses itself in independence from God. Extended further, the folly of human self-sufficiency is readily observable in the view that we are unaffected by systems and structures.

- Reinhold Niebuhr's activism and pastoral duties allowed him to observe, firsthand, the ways in which sin as pride took on a communal shape. He was keenly aware of how social groups—including racial groups—protected interests to the detriment of the vulnerable.

- Karl Rahner illustrates the social dimension of sin with an example of everyday commerce. He writes, "When someone buys a banana, he does not reflect on the fact that its price is tied to many presuppositions. To them belongs, under certain circumstances, the pitiful lot of banana pickers, which in turn is co-determined by social injustice, exploitation, or a centuries-old commercial policy. This person now participates in this situation of guilt to his own

---

common sense to the majority culture. On the other hand, I will also refer to the sensibilities of people of color who navigate a racialized world, knowing what they must do to survive and thrive. This kind of common sense can include ways of speaking or relating that should be encouraged or avoided, knowledge of what to expect in spaces perceived to be inhospitable, etc.

advantage."[19] Confronting racism as sin in the social dimension of human experience, then, requires a different approach than private discipleship and formation.

- Wolfhart Pannenberg warns against reducing the doctrine of sin to individual acts and asserts that individual life and social life are inextricably linked: "The former being always constituted by social relations, so sin works itself out in the social forms of life."[20] He elsewhere argues against individualistic "moralism" that obscures our solidarity in universal sinfulness with those who are captive to influences that induce them to further sinfulness.[21] If it can be established that racism has corrupted features of our social life, it stands to reason that we should expect its ongoing influence and its concrete expressions as ordinary.

- John Zizioulas emphasizes relationality with God and others as that which was disrupted in the fall. In Adam, other human beings cease to be subjects and become objects to us. That object is judged by us, the knower, regarding the worth of the object *to* us. In the midst of the "Great Resignation" of 2021, the popular mantra "Know your worth" reflects the situation in which we find ourselves. We measure ourselves and others not by our communion with God but by our productivity. Marginalized communities of color have been judged by the standards set by knowers of relative privilege, and those judgments can

19. Rahner, *Foundations of Christian Faith*, 110.
20. Pannenberg, *Systematic Theology*, 2:255.
21. Pannenberg, *Systematic Theology*, 2:238.

and have become our unspoken perspectives across difference.

Three observations are pertinent about this list of theological voices. First, I have not included those voices that propound interiority and highlight sin as individual act, nor have I highlighted the ways in which the theologians I *have* included treat interiority and *sin as act*. There is a place for all of these perspectives, and one would have to ignore the biblical text itself to deny their importance—as, I argue above, anti-structuralists do regarding the nonindividualist formulations of the doctrine of sin. In fact, the anti-structuralist foreclosure seems much more like a recent aberration against the backdrop of the millennia of theological formulation that have preceded. Hence, in a discussion about CRT, foregrounding *non*individualist accounts of sin opens up, rather than forecloses, possibilities for constructive engagement.

Second, Thiselton's list does not include voices of color and is somewhat dismissive of the feminist contributions from Valerie Saiving and Jackie Plaskow. What has preceded is an attempt to use oft-tread theological territory to demonstrate how Christians need not foreclose a meaningful engagement with systemic and structural matters. If the preceding theological voices do not create such space, I am not hopeful that voices of color will be more persuasive to skeptics. Nevertheless, voices of color and women's voices do articulate the dynamics of sin in ways that provide a ready bridge to CRT. (Frankly, in my judgment, so do the theological voices that I have highlighted above.)

Third, systems and structures can have a sin-sustaining capacity of their own that largely escapes the focus of the formulations above. For example, in Plantinga's culpability-focused conversation, he recognizes (as does Mohler) the role that systems play in misshaping humans who will go on to sin culpably. Culpability thinking enables us to hold individuals responsible for their actions. However, it also enables a knower to use a kind of prosecutorial discretion in which one may excuse a culpable individual since we are all misshapen by the systems and structures around us. This discretion, of course, often works in favor of those who share culpability with the knower. Few of the theological formulations above energize direct redress of the forces that misshape us, but there are alternatives with which we may engage constructively.

Chiefly, I would point to theological reflection in communities of color. Herein, formulations of the doctrine of sin *presuppose* thicker meaningfulness and centrality of community. These presumptions stand out against the backdrop of individualistic formulations. A few examples will illustrate this:

- Sri Lankan Jesuit Aloysius Pieris writes, "The stoic ideal of liberation was the *interior* emancipation of the human person from the *interior* bonds of spiritual slavery rather than release from external social structures of enslavement."[22] This interiority, for Pieris, explains the toleration of forms of oppression like slavery and caste.

- Feminist and postcolonial theologian Kwok Pui Lan observes that "people who live in traditional cultures as well as indigenous peoples know intimately that their actions have bearings on the natural environment, and not just on human history."[23] In order to

22. Pieris, *Asian Theology of Liberation*, 114–15.
23. Kwok, *Introducing Asian Feminist Theology*, 91.

be articulate about sin in all its forms, one cannot simply look to its effects in individual humans, nor can its scope be limited to human history.

- James H. Evans Jr. briefly reflects on sin in black theology vis-à-vis the theology of salvation. He writes, "Simply put, salvation required the seizing of one's freedom from whatever and whoever hindered human beings from becoming that which God created them to be. Likewise, sin is defined as the rejection of that demand."[24]

- Native American scholar Clara Sue Kidwell writes, "In Christianity, sin has become privatized as a personal matter. For Indian people it is a matter of responsibility to community. Those who do not participate in ceremonies with appropriate thoughts may negate the effectiveness of the ceremony to effect a restoration of appropriate relationships to restore the whole community to well being."[25] The communal, interpersonal relatedness of even private thought life works itself out in public, social experience.

- Similarly, Miguel De La Torre writes, "Regardless as to how private we may wish to keep sin, it always affects others because we are communal creatures. Hence, Hispanics maintain that sin has both an individual and a communal dimension."[26]

To the degree that Christian ethics and praxis are driven by confessional and theological commitments, concreteness

24. Evans, *We Have Been Believers*, 128.
25. Kidwell, Noley, and Tinker, *Native American Theology*, 110.
26. De La Torre and Aponte, *Introducing Latino/a Theologies*, 55.

and explicitness about the social (and ecological) dimensions of human sinfulness are important for meaningful mission and action.

In summary, while the ordinariness of sin is commonly granted, the scope and nature of sin is conceived variably. A narrowed scope that centers on individual, culpable actions and attitudes can more easily refuse approaches to racism that are ethically prescriptive regarding systems and structures that feel beyond the scope of the parochial, personal management of our own attitudes and actions. In fact, it should be said that hyper-privileging individual regeneration has granted Christians permission not only to treat social action as optional but also to dismiss such action as the business of the nonregenerate. If it were possible for Christians' best intentions to vanquish racism, then perhaps sincerity alone would have had a measurable impact by now. Alas, the opposite has shown itself to be the case. The plea here at the end of this brief consideration of the doctrine of sin is addressed to those who sincerely desire to combat racism in all its forms. As we move to consider the ordinariness of racism, focusing on one's private intentions and personal culpability diverts both the attention that is due those who suffer racial injustice and the energy for faithful action.

## Racism as Ordinary

"You are changing the definition!" A group of graduate students met with me weekly for lunch, Bible study, and prayer. As a pastor, I was always testing new ways of talking about race, justice, and reconciliation, and these intensely bright engineering students were an incredibly rigorous proving ground for my ideas. Over the weeks one student resisted the direction of our conversations. When we met to talk about his concerns, he made it clear that he viewed my treatment of the concept of racism as an agenda-driven innovation. He found it absurd that racism could be anything beyond personal animus toward someone of another race. His "common sense" about racism was very deep seated, and I could feel the ragged edges of my own relational shortcomings the longer we talked. We were unable to enter an examination of the premises that undergirded his view.

Since then, I have had countless conversations like that one. The time and energy required to get on the same page about what is meant by *racism* can be a serious barrier. But failure to try, in my experience, nearly guarantees greater polarization in a community. Furthermore, interiority and culpability thinking incline various audiences to hear and experience accusation and condemnation when discussions of racism take place. For example, I remember the look of disgust on the face of an elderly Christian man who had survived the Japanese internment camps as he leaped to criticize a diversity training that he felt cowed white Christians (whom he loved) into guilt over the United States' history of racial injustice. To be sure, some trainings and trainers weaponize guilt and end up exacerbating personal and ideological divides. Though skill and intentionality about learning outcomes vary widely, I think it is much less often the case that guilt-tripping is a deliberate tactic. I still trust that most trainers are aware that guilt is not a durable motivation.[27]

27. I have also seen the exasperation of trainers of good will who run face-first into the brick walls of racialized "common sense." The quicker that audiences perceive accusation and condemnation and begin to defend their narrow definitions, the more difficult the trainer's job becomes. It is common to hear talk of "fragility" among those who have encountered these perceptions as they try to shift a conversation to include forms of racism beyond personal, racial animus. Once it is perceived (rightly or wrongly) that someone is leveraging guilt to shift the conversation, the effort begins to crumble.

On a similar note, critical race theorists do not, contrary to the view of some pundits, seem to display much interest in generating guilt. This may be, in part, due to the scope of what can be intended by the concept of racism. That is, racism as personal attitudes and culpable actions is not at the center of their scrutiny and activism.[28] Rather, to aver that racism is ordinary reads more like the report of a finding than an anxious dogma. Just as many theologians are unsurprised to find the presence of *sin as act*, as well as all-pervading sinful*ness* throughout personal experience and social life, so are critical race theorists in legal studies not surprised to find the effects of racialized thinking in the foundational documents that establish American jurisprudence—and, by extension, social and political life in the United States. In fact, I encourage the reader to keep in mind what we discussed about the dynamics of sin and sinfulness in the previous section as we move ahead to describe the dynamics of racism in American social and political life.

Though the language of ordinariness is prominent in Richard Delgado and Jean Stefancic's *Critical Race Theory: An Introduction*, I have chosen to use the language of Eduardo Bonilla-Silva when framing racism because of the way it illuminates what is less visible. When his seminal paper on race theory was published in 1997, he forcefully objected to the way in which race was being framed as individual attitudes and beliefs (also referred to as *prejudice*)—the related problem in doctrinal imagination and formulation that I

---

28. It should be understandable at this point that when skeptical onlookers read the work of critical race theorists, individualistic formation may incline them to read personal condemnation in CRT—hence the inflamed interpretation that CRT attempts to make white people feel bad about being white. It is not clear to me that critical race theorists care about such feelings—at least not more than they care about reforming systems.

have attempted to elucidate above.[29] The following succinct restatements of his longer essay deserve further exploration and elaboration below:

1. "Racism is embedded in the structure of a society."
2. "Racism has a psychology, but it is fundamentally organized around a material reality (i.e., racism has . . . as a 'material foundation')."
3. "Racism changes over time."
4. "Racism has a 'rationality' (actors support or resist a racial order in various ways because they believe doing so is beneficial to them)."
5. "Overt, covert, and normative racialized behaviors (following the racial etiquette of a racial order) are all paths that 'racial subjects' have in any society."
6. "Racism has a contemporary foundation and is not a mere remnant of the past."[30]

Crucially, Bonilla-Silva contrasts a "structuralist" approach with an idealist one. Idealism, in sociology, "sees reality as ultimately composed of ideas rather than *a realm existing outside* human consciousness."[31] In 1997, Bonilla-Silva was critiquing the state of race studies for remaining in the realm of attitudes and beliefs. Twenty-five years later, Christian skeptics of CRT sometimes double down on an idealist conception of reality by appealing to what they call "worldview." Their concern, as mentioned previously regarding the Southern Baptist statement on CRT, is that a "transcendent ideological framework" is competing with

29. Bonilla-Silva, "Rethinking Racism."
30. Bonilla-Silva, "More than Prejudice," 76.
31. Hoffman, "Idealism," 277 (emphasis added).

the "biblical worldview."[32] Bonilla-Silva and other critical race theorists, however, are not doing their work in such an idealist frame. Instead, theirs is a much more "immanent frame" that merely feels foreign to the idealist.

In a structuralist account, phenomena can be ordinary when they are embedded in our lives, whether or not we are psychologically aware of them. There is some variation in what sociologists consider to be structures, but generally they include norms, values, roles, institutions, ways of relating, and the like. Some of the structures through which one might experience racism are becoming easier to name (e.g., discriminatory redlining in lending for home buyers), while others can be more difficult to observe. Take, for example, the school *system*, as we say in common parlance. The school system is made up of faculty, staff, and administrators. Importantly, the system is also shaped by policies, procedures, curricula, facilities, and so on. Because of the tacitly accepted meaning of *racism* in much of the viewing audience, the nightly news is likely to broadcast stories about an individual's racist conduct, or perhaps a clash between a school board and parents at the intersection of curricula, politics, and race. What often escapes popular public consideration are the effects of structuring school funding on the basis of property taxes. Over the last two decades, report after report has demonstrated that funding disparities disadvantage communities of color and poorer districts.[33]

32. The diversity of those who would criticize worldview thinking is impressive. Unfortunately, there is not enough space here for a direct treatment of the pitfalls of worldview thinking. For an appreciative and critical treatment, see Naugle, *Worldview*.

33. See, for example, Baker, Farrie, and Sciarra, *Is School Funding Fair?*

The eventual shift from racism as animus to racism as structural is one of the changes in how racism is studied and understood. For example, unless one discloses racist attitudes, choosing one's neighborhood, in part, because of its school district may seem like a completely practical and impersonal calculation. In fact, this kind of impersonal decision-making is what Chief Justice William Rehnquist assumed in *Pasadena City Board of Education v. Spangler*. Briefly, in 1954, *Brown v. Board of Education* led to the decree that schools be desegregated. In 1970, when it was found that the Pasadena schools were still segregated, the district was ordered to begin the process of rectifying this violation. For the first year, mandatory busing achieved a numerical racial balance in each school site, but busing became a contentious issue in the city. For the next few years, the district did not meet the same standard, setting the stage for the Supreme Court case. The oral arguments from both sides of the case make it clear that the situation in Pasadena was complex because the neighborhood demographics continued to change.

In several passages, Chief Justice Rehnquist wrote about those demographic changes and explicitly rejected the notion that "white flight" could be attributed to the decree that the district had to balance the racial population of the schools to comply with integration orders. The white population of Pasadena decreased from 82.7 percent in 1958 to 65.5 percent in 1965, and the black population of several school sites came to exceed 50 percent between 1970 and 1974. But these shifts did not stop Chief Justice Rehnquist from concluding that this was not "white flight" but rather a "quite normal pattern of human migration."[34] The creation of the La Cañada Unified School District and the rapid rise of private schools in this area—including evangelical ones—are clustered around this time frame too. Today, a whopping 36 percent of students in Pasadena attend private schools, reducing funding for their public school counterparts. In contrast, the public school district is 81.9 percent students of color, with 62.7 percent of public school students qualifying for free or reduced-price school lunch.[35]

What social structure is in question in the narrative above? There are numerous candidates, but I'll focus on one set of structures for its ordinariness and ubiquity: the value of home ownership (and all the laws, processes, and institutions associated with obtaining a home).[36] When my wife and I started searching for a home in Southern California, we were asked by well-meaning congregation members whether we were looking "north or south of the highway." We didn't realize that these two geographic designations were functionally code for neighborhoods that were either majority white or majority non-white. To this day, neighborhood-level census data reveal the persistence of cities' decades-long racial divides. This is an opportunity to illustrate what critical race theorists understand as the intractability of racism. Race has

34. Pasadena City Bd. of Educ. v. Spangler, 427 U.S. 424 (1976). See also Tom Wicker, "'Stifling' Pasadena's Integration," *New York Times*, April 29, 1973, https://www.nytimes.com/1973/04/29/archives/stifling-pasadenas-integration-in-the-nation.html.

35. "2021–22 PUSD Enrollment by Student Race/Ethnicity," CALPADS Fall 1.2 Norm Day Snapshot, accessed August 3, 2022, https://www.pusd.us/site/handlers/filedownload.ashx?moduleinstanceid=12689&dataid=19141&FileName=2021-22%20Enrollment%20by%20Ethnicity%20Trend.pdf. "Sex by School Enrollment by Type of School by Age for the Population 3 Years and Over," United States Census Bureau, 2019, https://data.census.gov/cedsci/table?q=School%20Enrollment&g=1600000US0656000&tid=ACSDT1Y2019.B14003.

36. We considered the illegal practice of redlining in chap. 1.

impacted the housing market for generations now. The value we place on homeownership, and all the benefits that accrue to homeowners of any social group, are quite stable. When they have a choice, families with means will continue to value and choose neighborhoods with highly rated schools. No one is shocked.

To point a critical gaze at the structural dynamics that culminate in school funding inequities and to search for remedies is to be less concerned with the attitudes and beliefs of individual home buyers. CRT's understanding of racism is one in which home buyers can be participants in a system that is unconcerned with the welfare of students of color and yet, without transgressing common sense, can hold privatized values related to their own welfare. To the degree that one treats housing choices as the uncomplicated "rationality" of the American Dream, one risks ignoring how their choices impact everything from food insecurity to environmental health and safety in other communities. Critical race theorists call systems and structures that do not deliberately consider outcomes for people of color "colorblind." To address this problematic color blindness, they advocate for policy making that is intentionally conscious of both the racially fraught histories of policy matters and the potential outcomes—especially for people of color.

To circle back to the beginning of this section, I understand why the grad student wanted to maintain a definition of racism that relegated it to the mistakes of our past. We are invested in the systems that we're helping to build and maintain, or from which we, our families, or our predecessors have benefited. In fact, the most cherished stories (fictive or otherwise) that form our sense of peoplehood spring forth from the blood, sweat, or tears of those whose legacies we feel are worth defending—always backed by the "power of the sword." The story that racism is now the exception and no longer the rule has been scaffolded upon egregiously selective readings of Rev. Dr. Martin Luther King Jr., appeals to idealized passages of the United States' founding documents, and even culturally conditioned characterizations of the person, work, and way of Jesus. New stories, including "counternarratives" from critical race theorists, demonstrate just how widespread and deeply rooted color-blind and individualist ideologies are. Wild mischaracterizations of CRT manifest the anxiety of myths in decline.

## Who Perceives Racism as Ordinary?

A few years ago, I attended an hours-long "racial reconciliation" workshop run by a local church. There were dozens of people, perhaps even a hundred, in attendance. Many of them were leaders in their congregation. Having experienced many kinds of diversity and inclusion workshops, I was familiar with the stories, simulations, and exercises. Sadly, the outcomes would also be familiar to me. Since then, I have encountered people who attended that workshop and were so deeply offended by the new narratives about themselves and their church, city, and country that they came away even more resistant than they had been before the workshop. One participant told many of his fellow church members that he was made to feel so badly about himself that he now feels like an utterly useless liability in the work of racial reconciliation. Another church member, so angered that the church would host such a workshop, furiously decried the contents of the training as nothing more than silly "hurt feelings."[37]

37. At this point, some might accuse me of prioritizing the "fragility" of the people who withered at this training. In reply, I would say that if the goal of training was to deepen racial resentment, this workshop succeeded. If, however, the

Even if individuals can bring themselves to believe or empathize with the testimony of people of color who experience racism, many well-intended Christians still have little to no exposure to the people and places with whom and where their noblest intentions could be tried. This is a recipe for ongoing disbelief and dismissal, for a consistently deaf ear to the cries of people in distress. Education scholars, using CRT, describe the work of telling one's own story as "validation" for oneself and one's community before a disbelieving wider world.[38] In other words, the chasm is wide when it comes to the awareness of the ordinariness of racism.

To some degree, "Racism is ordinary" constitutes part of the long-standing common sense of many people of color. In too many areas of human experience, people of color's experiences of racism create a different "common sense." For example, among African Americans who know about the Tuskegee Syphilis Experiment, 51 percent report less trust for medical researchers.[39] Black and Latina women experience "severe maternal morbidity" at disproportionate rates, leading to mistrust of medical professionals.[40] Asian Americans are increasingly aware of barriers they face to being promoted in the workplace.[41] When Pope Francis visited Canada in 2022, seeking repentance and reconciliation

---

goal was to create new opportunities for the narratives of people of color to shape congregational life, it failed. In fact, I would go even further and argue that many attendees are now inoculated against future attempts at having their narratives augmented or challenged. I believe this outcome makes congregational life worse for people of color who are attempting to make these spaces their ecclesial home.

38. Rivers et al., "That Wasn't My Reality," 343.

39. Shavers, Lynch, and Burmeister, "Knowledge of the Tuskegee Study," 567.

40. Howell et al., "Race and Ethnicity."

41. Buck Gee and Denise Peck, "Asian Americans Are the Least Likely Group in the U.S. to Be Promoted to Management," *Harvard Business Review*, May 31, 2018, https://hbr.org/2018/05/asian-americans-are-the-least-likely-group-in-the-u-s-to-be-promoted-to-management.

over emerging documentation of the historic abuse of the country's indigenous people, the Catholic Doctrine of Discovery was once again in the protest spotlight. The seizure of indigenous lands had been justified by this fifteenth-century doctrine, which has yet to be repealed. In most every conceivable area of social life in the United States, statistics *and* stories of the influence of race and racism abound—health outcomes, employment, housing, education, criminal justice, media representation, politics, and notably, congregational life.

Having worked in campus ministry since 2001, I have not seen the kind of exodus of young people of color from the church like I have seen since 2016. One group informed me that their church's failure to speak meaningfully after the police killings of black men was a kind of color blindness that disillusioned and dismayed them. Numerous groups of college students in the most diverse generations to date define themselves in opposition to white evangelicalism on more topics than just race. The work of "deconstruction" has led many young people to scrutinize the assumptions of traditional, Western doctrines (e.g., as was demonstrated above regarding the doctrine of sin). I have also listened as Christian leaders have contemptuously dismissed this deconstruction. They are unable to perceive the seriousness of the chasm that separates them from people they might otherwise serve.

In fact, this perception gap has been measured. The Public Religion Research Institute (PRRI) reports the following: "White Christians are generally less likely than other religious groups and the religiously unaffiliated to say that blacks experience significant discrimination. Only slightly more than one-third (36%) of white evangelical Protestants believe there is a lot of discrimination against blacks in the

U.S. today, while six in ten (60%) disagree."[42] PRRI also observed perception gaps regarding discrimination against immigrants and LGBTQ+ persons. I have heard white evangelical leaders report that there are no race problems in their overwhelmingly white denominations, or that discrimination against white evangelicals is as serious (or more serious) a problem as discrimination against other racial groups.[43] All this makes it "ordinary" for many people of color to expect color-blind ministry paradigms and theologies that do not reflect their experiences of God or their sense of what constitutes "good news." At the end of the day, if readers are still looking for a litany of phenomena to convince them about the ordinariness of racism in the United States and in their churches, they have not listened to the cries of those who experience racism. Furthermore, the perception gap is more than a relational gap. Though deep, diverse friendships are preferable to racial isolation for ethical formation on issues of race, there are other, more pervasive shaping influences at work. Critical race theory helps alert us to the place that law, in general, occupies in the American imagination and shapes even congregational life.

In the summer of 2020, anti-Asian racism was surging. While the stories I began to hear from friends and colleagues weren't thematically new, the frequency was beyond alarming. When it came my turn to face a congregation member who sought to defend the use of anti-Asian rhetoric, I knew

42. Daniel Cox, Rachel Lienesch, and Robert P. Jones, "Who Sees Discrimination? Attitudes on Sexual Orientation, Gender Identity, Race, and Immigration Status," *PRRI*, June 21, 2017, https://www.prri.org/research/americans-views -discrimination-immigrants-blacks-lgbt-sex-marriage-immigration-reform/.

43. Fifty-seven percent of white evangelicals say that Christians face a lot of discrimination. See Daniel Cox and Robert P. Jones, "Majority of Americans Oppose Transgender Bathroom Restrictions," *PRRI*, March 10, 2017, https://www .prri.org/research/lgbt-transgender-bathroom-discrimination-religious-liberty/.

that a relational approach would accomplish little. Instead, I was concerned about the environment that gave safe harbor and a wide berth to this member's (and many others') nationalist conduct. To reiterate, my concern was not primarily the attitudes and beliefs of individual church members but the systems and structures that allowed them to thrive and propagate—everything from the statement of faith and the bylaws to ministry strategies and leadership culture. I knew that the constitutional logic of protected speech already informed the discourse ethics of this congregation. In terms of leadership culture on church staffs, I also knew from experience that if an employee's conduct were clearly racially problematic but did not clearly violate a particular law, HR could function to protect the organization.

It is imperative to engage a church's systems and structures. When I can, I seek to engage the church's learning communities with the kind of comparative doctrinal analysis that I've included in this chapter. This has not been easy. Once, when I pointed out the individualistic leanings of our church's pietist doctrine, I was met with forceful resistance and consternation from a vocal few. I have also counseled churches to abandon the vague aspirations for diverse hiring that permit them to pass over candidates by appealing to a "culture fit." And when consulting on a church's liturgical culture, I ask systemic and structural questions about how the steady diet of worship elements are forming and shaping a congregation for racial justice. When preachers ask about homiletics, I often challenge them to point beyond culturally "relevant" sermon illustrations that further tokenize congregation members who are not part of the majority culture. Perhaps most difficult, I have suggested to congregations that church discipline protocols must account for the ordinariness of racism. I'll give an example in the section that follows.

## Matthew 18 Revisited

Church leaders who don't consider how shame works in biblical narratives sometimes take Matthew 18:15–20 as a rule book penned by the ancients to be cut and pasted in the relational conflicts we face from time to time. It is assumed that the "Matthew 18 protocol" can be characterized as follows:

Step 1: If you have been affronted by someone, it is your responsibility to do the supererogatory (i.e., going above and beyond the call of duty) thing and confront them directly. Hopefully your opponent will admit wrongdoing, and all will be resolved. (v. 15)

Step 2: If Step 1 does not work, take someone with you and repeat the process, for there is strength in numbers. Maybe it will be taken more seriously if two go, instead of one. (v. 16)

Step 3: If Step 1 and Step 2 do not work, get church leaders involved and consider expelling that person from your social group. Ideally, church discipline is meant to eventually restore. Practically, the process rarely gets this far before at least one party leaves. (v. 17)

This protocol reflects a hermeneutic that is more influenced by legal idealism and by affiliation by revocable consent than by biblical studies or covenant community commitments. Thankfully, there are more helpful readings of this text.

Craig Keener points out three historically rooted aspects of this passage.[44] First, Jesus's instruction is meant to avoid publicly shaming the offender. It seems right to me that this teaching is actually even more difficult for modern readers than my first characterization of it. Nevertheless, there are a few practices that even this reframing does not permit. Categorically burdening victims to enact justice for themselves is lopsided, to say the least. In my first characterization of the "protocol," there is a treacherously thin line between requiring supererogation and blaming the victim. This is especially true when there are uneven power dynamics (which, by the way, is not the kind of situation being addressed in Matt. 18). It defies pastoral reason for a church or ministry to *require*, as a matter of course, that an aggrieved party accept the burden of confronting the offending party alone.

Second, Jesus's instruction is to bring witnesses, not strength in numbers. This is not about coercive force. It is about what today we might call "documenting" the incident. It brings formality in truth-telling to what could otherwise degenerate into defamation and hearsay.

Third, Jesus's instruction is about the family of faith and those who are demonstrating that they are not a part of the family of faith by their resistance to the cries of pain. I have seen churches that functionally eliminate verse 17 from Jesus's teaching, and I have seen organizations that seem trigger-happy for excommunication. This teaching is not easy for us. While this reframing of Matthew 18 cannot seriously be considered CRT, it reflects the intentionally

44. Keener, *Gospel of Matthew*, 453–54.

race-conscious concerns of people who suffer the failures of a very ordinary and problematic procedure for church discipline.

## Conclusion: Resistance as Faithfulness

This chapter has attempted to juxtapose the doctrine of original sin and the assertion that racism is ordinary. Properly understood, neither statement contradicts the preciousness and dignity of individual persons. Denial of either, on the other hand, works at the expense of those who suffer the effects of sin and racism. One form of denial that I have labored to illuminate is the idea that racism is a thing of the past whose vestiges manifest among only the radically impolite. Instead, I have asserted that there are many for whom the experience of racism is as ordinary as human fallenness. But there is good news!

While Bonilla-Silva is correct that racism continues to evolve to avoid detection by ensconcing itself in new rationalities, we are not left without a witness. The very existence and persistence of communities of faith that have endured the ravages and innovations of racism bear witness to the love of God in Christ. As we argued in the previous chapter, community cultural wealth directs us away from thinking of communities that suffer racism as deficient only. Instead, the history and spirituality of families and communities that have suffered and overcome are a fuel—or a kind of capital—that fires the engines of ongoing faithfulness. Similar to the way in which God's people are enjoined to remember God's faithfulness, "resistance capital" is embedded in communal memory and storytelling. For Christians, these stories are infused with spiritual power for those who would submit themselves to their spiritual kin who have known overcoming.

# 3

# Redemption

## Critical Race Theory in Institutions

### Introduction

In anticipation and a dress rehearsal of John's vision of the New Jerusalem, where people gather from every language, tongue, tribe, and nation, the United States is experiencing a cultural diversity explosion. According to the apostle Paul in his famous speech to the Areopagus, it is God who sovereignly shapes the demographic and ethnic composition of every nation so that people "should seek God, and perhaps feel their way toward him and find him" (Acts 17:27 ESV). The diversity explosion of the United States is God's doing. In light of this scriptural truth and the results of the 2020 census, God is doing a new and special thing in the United States. The United States is in the early stages of a profound racial and ethnic "mestizaje" (mixing), in which cultural groups from every continent on the globe are freely blending in a historically unprecedented way.

From 2010 to 2020, the multiracial population of the United States grew 276 percent to 33.8 million people; the black or African American population increased from 38.9 million to 41.1 million.[1] The American Indian and Alaska Native population increased from 5.2 million in 2010 to 9.7 million in 2020—an 86.5 percent increase.[2] The Hispanic/Latino population climbed by 23 percent to 62.1 million, and the Asian American community—made up of those whose origins are in any of the original peoples of the Far East, Southeast Asia, or the Indian subcontinent, including, for example, Cambodia, China, India, Japan, Korea, Malaysia, Pakistan, the Philippine Islands, Thailand, and Vietnam,[3] together with mixed-race Asians—increased to 24 million. The white population, also made up of people with diverse ethnic origins in Europe, the Middle East, or North Africa, remained the largest race or ethnicity group in the United States, with 204.3 million people identifying as white alone and 235.4 million reporting white alone or in combination with another group. However, the white alone population

1. Nicholas Jones et al., "2020 Census Illuminates Racial and Ethnic Composition of the Country," United States Census Bureau, August 12, 2021, https://www.census.gov/library/stories/2021/08/improved-race-ethnicity-measures-reveal-united-states-population-much-more-multiracial.html.

2. "2020 Census Statistics Highlight Local Population Changes and Nation's Racial and Ethnic Diversity," United States Census Bureau, August 12, 2021, revised October 8, 2021, https://www.census.gov/newsroom/press-releases/2021/population-changes-nations-diversity.html; "2020 Census: Native Population Increased by 86.5 Percent," *Indian Country Today*, August 13, 2021, https://indiancountrytoday.com/news/2020-census-native-population-increased-by-86-5-percent.

3. Anna Purna Kambhampaty, "At Census Time, Asian Americans Again Confront the Question of Who 'Counts' as Asian. Here's How the Answer Got So Complicated," *Time*, March 12, 2020, https://time.com/5800209/asian-american-census/.

has decreased by 8.6 percent since 2010.[4] The Census Bureau projects that the multiracial population will triple by 2060,[5] and it is estimated that as much as 20 percent of the entire US population will be mixed-race by 2050.[6] In fact, in the near future, the growth of the mixed-race population will outpace that of Asians, Latinos, whites, blacks, and Native Americans.[7]

This diversity is also reflected in the changing demographics of the US church and Christian colleges and universities. According to Amos Yong, the dean of Fuller Seminary, the North American church is "browning" as white representation is declining and all other ethnic groups are together increasing.[8] White evangelical Protestants in the United States have experienced the most precipitous decline in affiliation since 2010, dropping from 23 percent to 14 percent.[9] Immigration from places such as Latin America, Africa, and Asia is fueling this rapid ecclesial change, and in fact, one in three American evangelicals is now a person of color. Accordingly, approximately one-quarter of all Christians

4. "2020 Census Statistics Highlight Local Population Changes."
5. Jonathan Vespa, Lauren Medina, and David M. Armstrong, "Demographic Turning Points for the United States: Population Projections for 2020 to 2060," United States Census Bureau, March 2018, revised February 2020, https://www.census.gov/content/dam/Census/library/publications/2020/demo/p25-1144.pdf.
6. "U.S. Census Bureau Projections Show a Slower Growing, Older, More Diverse Nation a Half Century from Now," United States Census Bureau, December 12, 2012, https://www.census.gov/newsroom/releases/archives/population/cb12-243.html. See also Vanessa Cárdenas, Julie Ajinkya, and Daniella Gibbs Léger, "Progress 2050: New Ideas for a Diverse America," Center for American Progress, October 18, 2011, https://www.americanprogress.org/article/progress-2050/.
7. Frey, *Diversity Explosion*, 4.
8. Yong, *Renewing the Church*, 24.
9. "PRRI Releases Groundbreaking 2020 Census of American Religion," *PRRI*, July 8, 2021, https://www.prri.org/press-release/prri-releases-groundbreaking-2020-census-of-american-religion/.

in the United States come from first-generation immigrant families.[10] As part of these rapid changes, Yong argues, grassroots expressions of church are "gradually displacing the Christendom that birthed theological education as we currently understand it."[11]

Reflective of these demographic changes in the US church, the student body composition of schools affiliated with the Council for Christian Colleges and Universities (CCCU) has also become increasingly diverse in the past decade. Close to half of CCCU institutions have more than 30 percent diversity in their student body, and from 2004 to 2019, the number of students of color increased by more than 14 percent. In the 2018–19 academic year, whites represented 58.5 percent of CCCU enrollment (a decrease of 9.28 percent from a decade earlier); Hispanic/Latino students composed 11.3 percent; African American / black students, 10.8 percent; Asian American / Pacific Islander students, 4 percent; and American Indian / Native American students, 0.5 percent.[12]

Although the Holy Spirit is birthing these dramatic changes in the US church and Christian colleges, seminaries, and universities, the senior leadership, faculty, staff, and curricula of these institutions largely reflect the church of fifty years ago. In order to keep step with the Spirit, revitalization of our seminaries and Christian colleges and universities requires curricular and structural overhaul. As Yong asserts, we need

10. Sarah Eekhoff Zylstra, "1 in 3 American Evangelicals Is a Person of Color," *Christianity Today*, September 6, 2017, https://www.christianitytoday.com/news /2017/september/1-in-3-american-evangelicals-person-of-color-prri-atlas.html; Yong, *Renewing the Church*, 14, 24.

11. Yong, *Renewing the Church*, 43.

12. "Diversity on CCCU Campuses," Council for Christian Colleges and Universities, accessed August 1, 2022, https://diversity.cccu.org/wp-content/uploads /2021/01/2021-CCCU-Diversity-Stats.pdf.

theological education that reflects the diverse cultural movement of the Spirit, or "of and from Pentecost."[13]

If, in accordance with sacred Scripture, the cultural makeup of nations is in fact an act of the sovereignty of God, and the church is intended to be God's primary interim vehicle moving humanity toward the beloved community of people of every tribe, language, nation, and tongue,[14] in this chapter we will ask, How should Christian institutions such as churches, denominations, nonprofit organizations, seminaries, and Christian colleges and universities respond to what God is doing in our midst? How might the theology of belonging articulated in chapter 1 serve as a road map for this task? In addition, how can intellectual tools from CRT, such as critical race counterstories, the voice of color thesis, and color blindness—together with their biblical corollaries— help us root out the obstacles that stand in the way of this heavenly dress rehearsal? Using the example of Christian higher education at both the seminary and the university level, this chapter will explore these important questions.

## The Voice of Color Thesis and the Changing Face of Seminary Education

I (Robert) can still hear the melodies and percussive rhythms of the Cuban *Guajira-son* guitar filling the sanctuary. Echoing

13. Yong, *Renewing the Church*, 35. To understand the history of race and whiteness in the structures of the US church, see Tisby, *Color of Compromise*. To learn more about the role of westward expansion and the Doctrine of Discovery in shaping the racialized systems of the US church, see Charles and Rah, *Unsettling Truths*. For an excellent discussion of racial liminality in the Asian American context, see Lee, *From a Liminal Place*. My (Robert's) own book, *Brown Church*, explores these same topics from a Latino vantage point. For a pathbreaking examination of the impact of such history on church worship practices, see Van Opstal, *Next Worship*.

14. Yong, *Renewing the Church*, 51.

the musical fusion of the African, Spanish, and indigenous in-fluences of the Buena Vista Social Club, the sixty-something-year-old *señoras* and *hermanos*, accompanied by one *joven* on conga, sang their hearts out in praise to Jesus. In the church basement below, we would later eat delectable se-lections of Caribbean dishes that this Mexican American from Los Angeles did not know the names of—but loved. In that same humble basement located in the heart of west Cleveland, the Galilean Theological Center (GTC) has been housed for the past sixteen years. I saw the future.

As previously discussed, one big conversation happen-ing today in seminary circles is about how much of con-temporary theological education is out of step with God's work in the quickly diversifying US church. Even though Protestant and evangelical churches in the United States are currently experiencing their greatest growth among believ-ers of Latino, Asian, and African descent, seminary educa-tion in 2021, as mentioned above, largely reflects the needs and ethnic composition of the church from fifty years ago. The GTC gave me a glimpse into the future and showed me how the theology of belonging articulated by John in Reve-lation 21:26 can be applied, in practical ways, in real time, to transform Christian higher education.[15] The GTC repre-sents organic Hispanic theological education housed in an immigrant church in the heart of an immigrant community.

Though Dr. Felix Muniz, founder and executive of the GTC, has had offers to move the school to more upscale locations, he insists on keeping it in the heart of the com-munity and literally within the local church. Because life in the community is hard and often requires full-time employ-ment from all family members to make ends meet, most do

15. To learn more about the GTC, see https://www.gtcohio.org.

not have the luxury of taking four years off from work to earn their undergraduate degree, and then another three to earn their graduate degree. The rigorous GTC diploma program offers them a creative on-ramp into seminary graduate studies. As part of this program, students take a wide range of courses grounded in Latina/o theology and *misión integral*, or holistic mission. According to René Padilla, who is credited with pioneering the concept of misión integral, this approach may be defined as "the mission of the whole church to the whole of humanity in all its forms, personal, communal, social, economic, ecological and political."[16]

Some of the classes offered include Writing and Research for Theological Study, The Call to Ministry, Tools for Biblical Interpretation, Survey of the Bible, Introduction to Hispanic Preaching, Hispanic Theology, History of the Hispanic Church, and Christian Education in the Hispanic Church. Courses are taught by leading educators in the local Cleveland area and leading Latina/o theologians from throughout the United States. In partnership with Ashland Theological Seminary, GTC graduates earn a diploma in theology and church ministry. Qualified graduates, moreover, are able to continue their graduate studies at Ashland Theological Seminary, Fuller Theological Seminary, Gordon-Conwell Theological Seminary, and various other seminaries across the country. GTC graduates over the past fifteen years number in the many dozens and have gone on to lead churches in major denominations and nonprofit organizations, pursue doctoral work, find stable employment in information technology and other fields, as well as find God's healing from broken family structures and freedom from addiction. The GTC offers a powerful example of the way seminary education can

16. Yamamori and Padilla, *Local Church*, 9.

be reshaped around the principle of the glory and honor of the nations in terms of leadership, curriculum, and holistic mission.

The GTC is part of a larger national movement of Hispanic theological education reform led by the Association for Hispanic Theological Education (Asociación para la Educación Teológica Hispana, AETH).[17] Founded in 1992 by noted theologian Justo González, AETH is a network of dozens of Latino seminaries and Bible institutes in the United States, Canada, Puerto Rico, Latin America, and the wider Caribbean that is dedicated to the promotion and improvement of Hispanic theological education. AETH sponsors annual conferences, communities of practice, and monthly *conversatorios*, and it partners with the Association of Theological Schools to create unique on-ramps into theological education for the Hispanic church community. Also sharing a genealogy tracing back to González, the Hispanic Theological Initiative and the Hispanic Summer Program are creative projects aimed at the diversification of Hispanic theological research in the doctoral and academic echelons.

According to Elizabeth Conde-Frazier, the executive director of AETH, Latinx theological education is a continuum that begins in various forms as Christian education at the local church and extends to Bible institutes, Christian colleges, and seminaries.[18] As reflected in the experimental example of the GTC, Latinx theological education is also currently in transition, as "two eras of theological education are overlapping, interrelating, and coinciding," and new educational design and experimentation is taking place to meet the needs of the current changing moment.[19] Drawing from

---

17. For more information on AETH, see https://www.aeth.info.
18. Conde-Frazier, *Atando Cabos*, 2.
19. Conde-Frazier, *Atando Cabos*, 1.

the metaphor of sewing, Conde-Frazier argues that we are in a time of *atando cabos sueltos*—repurposing previously unused textile fragments that had seemed out of place but are now becoming the basis for the new garment of Hispanic theological education. Her imagery of "tying up loose ends" recalls Jesus's much-quoted words in Matthew 9:16: "No one sews a patch of unshrunk cloth on an old garment, for the patch will pull away from the garment, making the tear worse."

According to Conde-Frazier, the theological frameworks of the priesthood of all believers and misión integral (holistic mission) are the *cabos sueltos*—or loose ends—that must shape our understanding of church and its mission and must be the drivers of the purpose of theological education for the Latina/o church.[20] The focus of this new era of Hispanic theological education, moreover, should no longer be the discussion of abstract concepts floating in a supposedly dehistoricized context but should be the preparation of a priesthood of believers for holistic mission. "The loci of our theological education are the lakes and oceans of our lives, the intersection of the practical and the theoretical as we move toward pastoral action."[21]

Applying a different metaphor to make a similar point, González argues that theological education is more akin to an irrigation hose than to a pipeline. For González, the ultimate goal of theological education is not a PhD pipeline that produces scholarship divorced from the life of the church and the daily lives of its members. Although such scholarship does have a role, González says, "The primary purpose of theological education is to help each believer irrigate the land

20. Conde-Frazier, *Atando Cabos*, 31.
21. Conde-Frazier, *Atando Cabos*, 72.

where she or he happens to be. Those who do not go beyond Sunday school, if they irrigate the land around them, are just as valuable as those who teach in a seminary or school of theology. And those who teach in such institutions are to be valued on the basis of how well they irrigate the land in which they have been placed."[22]

The examples of AETH and the GTC, as well as the unique insights of González and Conde-Frazier into the proper goals of theological education, offer a compelling illustration of what critical race theorists call the "voice of color thesis." According to the voice of color thesis, we people of color are in the best position to understand our own racialized experiences in the United States and to craft solutions. In the words of Richard Delgado and Jean Stefancic, "Because of their different histories and experiences with oppression, black, American Indian, Asian, and Latina/o writers and thinkers may be able to communicate to their white counterparts matters that the whites are unlikely to know."[23] For example, as a local Latino pastor and educator, Felix Muniz of the GTC was in the best position to understand the theological and pastoral needs of the Latina/o community of Cleveland. He understood the daily struggles of the people and what types of pastoral and theological education could best equip local pastors to serve in the community. He also understood the financial and structural roadblocks that placed a seminary education out of reach for most. And another example: in light of their combined experience of more than a century in Hispanic theological education and

22. Justo González, "There's No Theological Education Pipeline Anymore," *Christian Century*, December 23, 2020, https://www.christiancentury.org/article/how-my-mind-has-changed/there-s-no-theological-education-pipeline-anymore. For further reading on the development of theological education over the centuries, see González, *History of Theological Education*.

23. Delgado and Stefancic, *Critical Race Theory*, 10.

pastoral ministry in white and Latino contexts throughout the United States and Latin America, González and Conde-Frazier are optimally positioned to understand the curricular and institutional changes that are necessary to best train and empower Latina/o clergy in God's mission.

The voice of color thesis is entirely consistent with a biblical understanding of the body of Christ. Flowing from our unique God-given cultural treasuries and our peculiar histories and experiences of oppression in the United States, we Christians of color form distinctive parts of the body of Christ and uniquely reflect the image of God (Gen. 1:26–28; Rom. 12:4–5; 1 Cor. 12:12–14, 18–19). As such, one important role we play is as communicators of racial issues to our white sisters and brothers in the body of Christ who are unlikely to know about racial injustice from firsthand experience. It is necessary to state this clearly because our voices have so often been dismissed. Our perspectives are not better than others, yet flowing from our experiences as unique children of God, they are distinct. Rejecting our perspectives is akin to the eye saying to the hand, "I don't need you!" or the head telling the feet, "I don't need you!" (1 Cor. 12:21). At the same time, Christians of color cannot reject membership and participation in the body of Christ. Although sometimes tempting, it is not an option. To do so would be like a foot proclaiming, "Because I am not a hand, I do not belong to the body" or an ear saying, "Because I am not an eye, I do not belong to the body" (vv. 15–16). No, God has placed us each in the body just where he wants us to be (v. 18). We belong to and need one another in order to "reach unity in the faith and in the knowledge of the Son of God and become mature, attaining to the whole measure of the fullness of Christ" (Eph. 4:13; see also Rom. 12:5; 1 Cor. 12:21). In the words of Yong, "We need the many voices resonating in the cosmic cosmopolis because they bring with them many practices and capacities to resonate with the rule and reign of God in many glocal contexts."[24]

## Critical Race Counterstories and Reactionary Color Blindness

Color blindness silences the diverse voices of the cosmic cosmopolis. As will be illustrated through the following critical race counterstory, color blindness does not truly value the distinct perspectives brought by voices of color according to God's design, and so it often perpetuates leadership structures and approaches that maintain the racial status quo and hinder the diversification of Christian institutions. In the name of color blindness, and as a token nod to superficial appreciation of diversity, some predominantly white Christian colleges, seminaries, and nonprofit organizations hire people of color who think and act just like majority culture and who do not challenge the racial status quo. Such hiring practices may allow them to mark off their diversity checkbox and may give them a basis on which to claim that they are not prejudiced, but it leaves the racialized structures of their institutions fundamentally unchanged. At the same time, leaders of color who authentically minister out of the distinct perspectives that flow from their God-given "glory and honor" are often the first to lose their jobs, the last to be promoted, and the least likely to be hired. Many Christian institutions want the color of our skin in their pews and classrooms but are not truly interested in the perspectives that flow from journeying with Jesus in a different shade of skin.

24. Yong, *Renewing the Church*, 62.

As an entry point for the discussion of color blindness, I offer a CRT counterstory involving my recruitment for an executive-level position at a Christian university. Counter-stories can involve composite characters drawn from social science data, interviews, and personal experience. They are used to bring to light the personal and corporate experiences and perspectives of people of color that often run counter to dominant cultural narratives about minority populations. They are used to dispel myths and stereotypes and are similar in form and function to the parables of Jesus. Like Jesus's parables, they are used to point out social problems and uplift the experiences and perspectives of those left out of majority discourse.[25]

Several years ago, I was invited to apply for an executive-level administrative diversity position at a Christian university. After much prayer and reflection, I thought I should at least put my hat in the ring. I was excited by the opportunity to integrate my years of experience of teaching and leadership within the secular academy with my pastoral experience of training and mobilizing students, professors, campus ministries, and local churches in issues of race, diversity, and Christianity. I thought to myself, What a dream it would be to live an integrated life of ministry and academic vocation and to help shepherd a Christian university in issues of diversity and inclusion from a Christ-centered and biblical perspective!

I had had the privilege of participating in leading academic diversity programs and was inspired by the prospect of bringing such models to the CCCU and integrating them with a Christian worldview. I myself am a product of the Ford Foundation Predoctoral and Postdoctoral Fellowships,

25. Solórzano and Yosso, "Critical Race Methodology," 33.

as well as of the University of California President's Postdoctoral Fellowship Program. Through these long-standing and outstanding diversity programs, I have learned the best practices with respect to both professorial and graduate student diversity development and mentorship. I have also acquired a broad network of connections to diverse leading scholars from throughout the nation at colleges and universities ranging from Harvard, Yale, Brown, and the University of California to the Claremont Colleges and the CCCU. With respect to diversity and inclusion research and scholarship, I have published widely on issues related to race, history, law, education, and Christianity, including two nationally award-winning books (in both the secular academic and theological realms). I hold a PhD in Latin American history from UCLA and a JD from Berkeley. I am an attorney and have served on the editorial boards of the top academic journals in law, history, and ethnic studies in the nation. And I am a national speaker on issues of race and Christianity. I say these things not to boast but to provide context for the counterstory I am sharing.

As I talked about this opportunity with friends from Christian colleges and seminaries, I was often met with hesitancy. Many had had bad experiences trying to engage the Christian world of higher education around issues of race and systemic transformation. The boards of trustees, faculty, and administrators of the Christian universities and seminaries they worked for were overwhelmingly white and male and had expressed resistance to structural change. I heard their concerns, but I wanted to give this Christian university the benefit of the doubt. As I moved along in the process, I was told repeatedly by the search firm that this university was serious about change and had been building up to the step of a serious diversity hire for many years. I was especially impressed by the culturally diverse hiring committee of more than a dozen people representing faculty, staff, and administrators across the large campus. It wasn't just talk or window dressing, the search firm assured me. They wanted real change. And I listened. And I believed them.

Daily for four months, I and my family prayed about this opportunity and how it might reshape everything about our life and ministry. I put most of my academic commitments on hold during this time as well. We gave it our all because this was a game changer for us, and we needed to be sure that this was God's will. Before long, I was a semifinalist, and not long after that, I became one of two finalists for the position. Was God opening the door? It was hard to contain my excitement. My intensive on-campus interview went very well, as far as I could tell. All the signs and signaling from those at the university—from the faculty to the president— seemed to indicate that it was going to happen.

And then, several days later, I received a seemingly sheepish call telling me that the position had been offered to someone else. It seemed to be a surprise to everyone, including the search firm. After the initial shock set in, I was devastated. What had happened?

In hindsight, there were some serious warning signs during the interview—some of which I can share publicly, and others that I do not feel would be ethically appropriate to share. Something just didn't smell right. The warning signs that I will discuss exemplify many of the barriers that hinder Christian colleges, universities, and seminaries from keeping step with the Spirit's work in the US church. In what follows, I will draw from my personal experience—my counterstory— and from the CRT frameworks of reactionary color blindness and the voice of color thesis to analyze some of these common barriers to the diversification of Christian colleges and seminaries, local churches, denominational leadership, and nonprofit organizations and parachurch ministries.

*Red Flag 1: Racial Passivity and Lack of Sincere Commitment to Diversity, Equity, and Inclusion.* In my conversation with one senior campus leader, I mentioned that although the level of student body diversity was strong on the campus, the issue of faculty diversity was a significant concern. I noted that UCLA's faculty was twice as diverse as the faculty at this Christian university. I also shared my ideas for faculty diversification in light of my positive experiences with programs like the Ford Foundation and the UC President's Postdoctoral Fellowship Program. How amazing it would be to create a pipeline of recruitment for faculty of color in the CCCU based on these models in the "secular world" that have been producing positive results for decades. In response, I was told that they thought faculty diversity would naturally flow from a diverse student body. Every bone in my body knows that this is not true. In fact, five decades of social scientific research in education proves the opposite point. As will be discussed further below, this passive approach evinces an opposition to the proactive creation of programs designed to improve diverse, equitable representation in the faculty and administrative leadership of Christian colleges and universities.

*Red Flags 2 and 3: Lack of Transparency and Resistance to Outside Accountability; Hostile Campus Climate for Students of Color.* This university had recently had a diversity audit conducted by, ironically, UCLA. Since I could not track down the findings of this audit online, I asked the search committee for a summary of the audit. I was told that the faculty and staff did not even know the details of the audit because the findings had not been publicly released. It was also shared with me that the university disagreed with the metrics utilized by the UCLA audit to measure its diversity; the school claimed that it was doing a better job at diversity than was reported by the audit. In addition, when I met with students of color during the campus interview, there was much pain in their eyes and in the stories they shared. They expressed concerns of a racial climate that was largely inhospitable to their perspectives and experiences.

*Red Flag 4: Racially Monolithic Senior Cabinet.* Another concern had to do with the cultural makeup of the existing senior leadership and the decision-making structure of the university. Members of the senior administration with whom I met were almost exclusively white. I do not recall a single Latina/o or Asian American senior administrator. To give them the credit they deserve, they also seemed to be earnest about the desire for increased racial diversity in the university ranks. Some were "woke," and most acknowledged that diversity was a needed biblical goal that they were seeking guidance in how to pursue—only a minority seemed resistant. One person made a negative and uninformed comment about CRT, but I was willing to let that slide. I was also bluntly honest with them when I said, "If you are not really open to 'going there,' please do not hire me. It would be a travesty for me to leave UCLA to come to an institution that was not serious about change." One administrator replied that they could not afford to not go there. And a board of trustees member seemed to concur.

*Red Flag 5: Disregard for Democratic Processes and Voices of Color.* At the end of the exhaustive search process, one troubling signal also occurred that forecast the final decision to be made. Though the diverse hiring committee recommended my name be put forward as the single finalist for the position, the senior leader charged with making the decision did not agree. He instructed the committee to include the name of an internal candidate on the list of finalists. In the end, a decision was made that would lead to the maintenance of the racial status quo on this particular campus.

Unfortunately, as Peter Rios, senior organization development consultant and executive coach at Harvard University, examines in *Untold Stories: The Latinx Leadership Experience in Higher Education*,[26] my negative experience with the hiring process in Christian higher education fits a larger, consistent pattern. Drawing on rigorous social scientific analysis and critical race storytelling—or counterstories—Rios's study is the first of its kind to faithfully, and honestly, share the stories of Latina/o administrators in the CCCU system. Also drawing on his own experience and on interviews with the senior Latinx administrators who have managed to scale the ranks of Christian higher education, he provides multitudinous examples of the institutional barriers, challenges, and racial microaggressions they have endured. In one "untold story," he shares about his own experience of witnessing well-qualified faculty and administrative candidates of color passed over by presidents and search committees who instead hired less qualified white candidates who were viewed as better "mission fits" or as less "prophetic."[27] Moreover, Rios states that he "witnessed over and over how the leadership would always make modifications for the majority culture in their hiring practices" as a form of affirmative action for white people.[28] He describes one especially pernicious incident at a Hispanic-serving institution in which one well-qualified Latino candidate was passed over for the position of dean of business in favor of a white female candidate with lesser qualifications: "I served on several search committees

26. Rios, *Untold Stories*.
27. Rios, *Untold Stories*, 6–8.
28. Rios, *Untold Stories*, 6.

and cabinet interviews that seemed to ignore highly qualified candidates of color. In one instance, when searching for a dean of business, the search committee did not want a particular Latino in this position because, according to them, he was not qualified enough, although he held a Ph.D. in a business field, was the chair of a business department, and had the business experience to qualify him. Subsequently, a White woman who had no education in business was chosen."[29]

In this instance, purportedly race-neutral reasons were given for not hiring the Latino candidate. This gave the hiring committee legal, and perhaps moral, cover. After denying the Latino candidate based on race-neutral justifications, this same committee, not understanding the transparency of their hypocrisy, chose to hire the white candidate who was less qualified than the Latino candidate on the basis of those exact same race-neutral factors. In other words, the supposedly race-neutral reasons used to exclude the candidate of color were used to mask invidious racial intent. Variations of this same tactic occur in faculty searches and pastoral selection committees across the United States. As a smoke screen for race, committees will say things like

He is too "divisive" or "political."

There just aren't enough Latinos with PhDs.

We're looking for someone who has not made "political statements" on social media (i.e., has not spoken out on racial issues such as police brutality, immigration reform, or educational inequality).

She has a problem with "authority."

He's qualified, but I question how grounded in the faith he is because he believes in CRT.

29. Rios, *Untold Stories*, 7.

The end result is that many highly qualified candidates of color get passed over unless they assimilate into the cultural norms and perspectives of predominantly white institutions. Stated simply, they must "become white" to be hired and accepted. If they do not, a myriad of race-neutral excuses can always be devised as a proxy for what amounts to, in the end, racial exclusion. In the political realm, Ted Cruz and Marco Rubio are examples of politicians who have chosen the path of assimilation to receive white acceptance by supporting policies that harm the vast majority of Latinas/os in the United States. Widespread support of Donald Trump on the part of many Latina/o evangelicals, such as Guillermo Maldonado and Samuel Rodriguez, offers a counterpart in the ecclesial community.

According to education scholars Alice Obenchain, William Johnson, and Paul Dion, a "clan culture" helps explain such racialized exclusion and the dearth of Latinos and other people of color in executive leadership positions within Christian higher education.[30] According to such a clan culture, ethnic minorities, women, and other recent arrivals to the world of Christian higher education—no matter how qualified—are prohibited from entering the inner (racial) circles. This certainly resonates with my experience at the local Christian university. Related to this clan mentality, and drawing from his interviews with senior Latinx administrators, Rios argues that the lack of equitable Latinx representation reflects the continuing structural inequities, biases, racism, and lack of genuine commitment to diversity, equity, and inclusion that permeate many Christian colleges and universities. In this sense, the broader philosophical and political alignment of much of Christian higher education

30. Obenchain, Johnson, and Dion, "Institutional Types," 32, 34–36.

with right-wing antidiversity ideologies and movements has the natural effect of stymying diversity efforts in the realm of Christian higher education.

## Color Blindness

In both positive and negative ways, a philosophical precommitment to color blindness was likely an implicit assumption of the provost with whom I interviewed. Perhaps he would have defended his hiring decision by saying that he doesn't "see" color, so institutional racism could not have been a factor. In a positive sense, he would affirm that all people are equal and created in the image of God, regardless of their cultural heritage, and that God does not have favorites. This aspect of contemporary Christian color blindness obviously aligns with scriptural truth and represents a big improvement from sixty years ago, when many white Christians confidently argued that they were racially superior to all other ethnic groups and that God condoned the "segregation of the races." Over the past five years, it has been sad to see some white, and even some Latino, Christians reverting back to such hellish theology, but I have no reason to believe that the provost in my example is of that persuasion. The positive sense of color blindness lines up squarely with Paul's words in the book of Galatians: "So in Christ Jesus you are all children of God through faith, for all of you who were baptized into Christ have clothed yourselves with Christ. There is neither Jew nor Gentile, neither slave nor free, nor is there male and female, for you are all one in Christ Jesus. If you belong to Christ, then you are Abraham's seed, and heirs according to the promise" (3:26–29).

Amen. Indeed, though the world tries to create modern-day ethnic caste systems and some Christians proffer pecking orders of God's favor along the lines of ethnicity, class, and gender, Paul teaches that this is not so in the economy of God. We are all children of God in Christ through faith, are heirs according to God's promise to Abraham that the entire world would be blessed through him, and are equal in the sight of God and one another.

While I can fairly confidently assert that the provost would hold to this biblical sense of color blindness, I can also deduce that he possessed a deficient view of color blindness insofar as he did not seem to appreciate the critical leadership benefits that flow from diverse cultural representation. Stated differently, he lacked a biblical understanding of the positive benefits of cultural diversity and community cultural wealth, which we discussed above in chapter 1. Otherwise, he would not have nonchalantly declared that the faculty, and presumably senior leadership, of Christian colleges and universities would naturally diversify over time without proactive measures. If pushed, he might have said that because he is color-blind, it doesn't matter what ethnic background an administrator comes from, because cultural heritage makes no net contribution to leadership. His likely possession of a philosophical precommitment to color blindness prevented him from envisioning or fully appreciating the positive transformation that his university could experience if opened up to the diverse, God-given cultural perspectives and leadership of those who differ from himself and who represent different parts of the body of Christ. He did not possess a biblical understanding of the glory and honor of the nations and seemed confident in his ignorance. In this sense, the provost was truly "blind" to the diverse cultural gifts of the Spirit. Flowing from this reasoning, it makes sense that he did not think that the cultural diversification of Christian colleges and universities was an urgent matter requiring creative solutions. Also predictable was his lack of openness to exploring—and adapting to his own context—successful programs of diversification, such as those developed by the Ford Foundation, the UC President's Postdoctoral Fellowship, the Bill and Melinda Gates Foundation, and other leading proponents of educational diversity over the past fifty years. Color blindness kept him—and keeps millions of others—from *seeing* the "new thing" that God is doing as God brings people from every tribe, language, nation, and tongue to the US church and, by extension, to its corollary educational institutions.

> *See*, I am doing a new thing!
>    Now it springs up; do you not perceive it?
> I am making a way in the wilderness
>    and streams in the wasteland.
>                    Isaiah 43:19, emphasis added

## Reactionary Color Blindness

Color blindness is harmful not only because it deprives us of the diverse leadership needed to successfully navigate our current racial moment but also because it denies, and thereby perpetuates, racialized structures of inequality in the United States. CRT scholar Ian Haney López refers to this as "reactionary" color blindness.[31] As with the provost of our previous example, reactionary color blindness opposes proactive measures aimed at remedying the effects of past racial injustice and denies the present existence of structural or systemic racism. It goes further, however, by creating a false moral equivalence between explicitly racist laws and

31. Haney López, "'Nation of Minorities,'" 985, 989.

policies of the Jim Crow era and contemporary laws and policies aimed at fostering greater opportunity for ethnic minorities. According to Haney López, such reactionary color blindness misappropriates the language of the civil rights movement in order to maintain the racial status quo and preserve the privileged socioeconomic and political privilege of whites in the United States: "[Color blindness] self-righteously wraps itself up in the raiment of the civil rights movement . . . and defines discrimination strictly in terms of explicit references to race. . . . Thus, it is 'racism' when society uses affirmative race conscious measures to respond to gross inequalities, but there is no racial harm no matter how strongly disparities in health care, education, residential segregation, or incarceration correlate to race, so long as no one has uttered a racial word."[32] The logic, or illogic, of reactionary color blindness goes something like this: "We should no longer consider color or ethnic heritage as a factor in employment, educational admissions, or government contracts, because we are all the same. Martin Luther King Jr. had it right—racial segregation and discrimination were wrong (even though most Christians opposed him at the time). Thankfully, racism is a thing of the past and no longer exists on a structural or systemic level in our churches, seminaries, colleges, public education system, health care system, or elsewhere. Where it does exist, it's usually against whites as reverse discrimination. Because structural racism does not exist, laws and policies designed to foster equal opportunities for ethnic minorities are unnecessary and constitute 'preferential treatment.' Two wrongs don't make a right, and laws designed to help minorities are just as bad as the laws that condoned slavery, segregation,

32. Haney López, *White by Law*, xviii.

and discrimination. I'm not racist, but I think that Hispanics and blacks need to stop making excuses, living off government welfare, and being so lazy."

Because color blindness does not value the distinct contributions of faculty of color and fails to recognize the persistence of educational inequality, it rests content in the fact that, for example, the overwhelming majority of CCCU faculty members—83.8 percent—are still white. It also does not view faculty diversification as an urgent priority, even though fewer than 3 percent are Hispanic/Latino; just 4.4 percent are African American; 4.6 percent are Asian American; and 0.3 percent are Native American. For similar reasons, color blindness is not disturbed by the fact that whites represent 84.4 percent of administrators at CCCU institutions, while only 4.1 percent are Hispanic/Latino, 5.2 percent are black, 3.1 percent are Asian American, and 0.3 percent are Native American. To adherents of color-blind theology, if racism exists at all, it is something that occurs only on a personal level between individuals, and the cultural heritage of administrators offers no critical leadership benefits. It is no wonder, then, that the lack of equitable cultural representation is viewed as unproblematic by so many. Color blindness wrapped in diversity language often conceals the operation of systemic racism on CCCU campuses.[33]

As a detrimental testimony to a watching world, color blindness helps explain why the number of administrators of color who work at secular institutions is twice the number of those working at religiously affiliated higher education institutions. It also contributes to the perception of many Christian colleges and universities as "safe havens" for white people, where color blindness is officially touted and where

33. Rios, *Untold Stories*, 59.

values such as individualism and Eurocentrism are conveyed as part of the hidden or unofficial curriculum.[34]

Noted black theologian Willie Jennings has expressed similar concerns related to the stated and unstated goals of traditional theological education in the United States. In *Beyond Whiteness*, he writes that Western theological education currently faces a crisis of belonging because of its promotion of a culturally homogeneous vision steeped in whiteness and American nationalism. As such, it results in the distorted formation of individuals in the "image of a white, self-sufficient man . . . defined by possession, control, and mastery."[35] In the spirit of CRT, Jennings argues that the roots of such distorted spiritual formation trace back to colonialism and the long history of white hegemony in this country.[36]

Unfortunately, the limited racial vision described by Jennings often extends beyond the seminary walls. As Latinos in the US church, we often feel like extras in a movie or add-ons or afterthoughts, whether in a sermon, a conference speaker lineup, a pastoral search, or the hiring process for a new position at the local seminary or Christian college. But we are God's children too. We are one of the tribes (Rev. 7:9). We belong equally to the family of God, and our cultural treasure and wealth is likewise of eternal value (Rev. 21:26).

The white cultural homogeneity discussed by Jennings and analyzed by Rios in the context of Christian higher education has been buttressed throughout US history by the social and theological construction of "white Jesus."[37] In their book, *White Jesus: The Architecture of Racism in Reli-*

---

34. Rios, *Untold Stories*, 25, 56–57; Conde-Frazier, *Atando Cabos*, 49.
35. Jennings, *After Whiteness*, 6.
36. Jennings, *After Whiteness*, 7.
37. Jennings, *After Whiteness*, 7; Rios, *Untold Stories*, 36.

*gion and Education*, Christian education scholars Alexander Jun, Tabatha Jones Jolivet, Allison Ash, and Christopher Collins argue that "white Jesus" is a historical social construction of white Christian empire that is used to justify white supremacy, patriarchy, and unrestrained capitalism. "White Jesus was constructed by combining empire, colorism, racism, education, and religion—and the byproduct is a distortion that reproduces violence in epistemic and physical ways."[38] In light of this understanding, it is perhaps not surprising that a giant thirty-foot mural of white Jesus adorns the campus that is home to some of the most vociferous and uninformed theological opposition to CRT that exists among Christian faculty. Jun and his coauthors are sure to differentiate white Jesus from the Jesus of the Gospels, "the one whose life, death, and resurrection demands sacrificial love as a response" and who inspires his followers to "do good; seek justice, rescue the oppressed, defend the orphan, plead for the widow."[39]

## Acts 6 as an Antidote to Reactionary Color Blindness

I close with one final takeaway from my critical race counterstory related to leadership structures and decision-making. Because, as has been discussed, reactionary color blindness does not see the inherent value in the distinct perspectives brought by people of color, it can perpetuate leadership structures and approaches that maintain the racial status quo and hinder the diversification of Christian institutions. In my case, the Christian university at hand thoughtfully

38. Jun et al., *White Jesus*, 20.
39. Jun et al., *White Jesus*, xx.

charged a diverse leadership team of faculty and staff to conduct a national search for a vice president of diversity who would help usher in needed structural change. After months of meetings and careful deliberation, their will was overridden in one fell swoop by a lone white senior administrator. This administrator and the larger institutional apparatus that enabled him ran afoul of the principles of leadership and ethnic reconciliation embodied by the early church in Acts 6. To utilize the language of CRT, his decision ran afoul of the voices of color principle.

In Acts 6:1–7, we are told that an ethnic conflict arose between Hellenistic Jews now residing in Jerusalem and their compatriot Hebraic Jews over the distribution of church resources:[40]

> In those days when the number of disciples was increasing, the Hellenistic Jews among them complained against the Hebraic Jews because their widows were being overlooked in the daily distribution of food. So the Twelve gathered all the disciples together and said, "It would not be right for us to neglect the ministry of the word of God in order to wait on tables. Brothers and sisters, choose seven men from among you who are known to be full of the Spirit and wisdom. We will turn this responsibility over to them and will give our attention to prayer and the ministry of the word."
>
> This proposal pleased the whole group. They chose Stephen, a man full of faith and of the Holy Spirit; also Philip, Procorus, Nicanor, Timon, Parmenas, and Nicolas from Antioch, a convert to Judaism. They presented these men to the apostles, who prayed and laid their hands on them.
>
> So the word of God spread.

40. Jennings, *Acts*, 65.

In this instructive example from the earliest church, we find that ethnic conflict in the church is normative. In this case, immigrant diaspora Jews who chose to remain in Jerusalem after Pentecost felt that their elderly widows were being overlooked by their Judean cousins in the daily distribution of food.[41] Similar ethnic conflicts over resources persist to the present day in local churches, denominations, seminaries, and Christian colleges and universities. In the case of the CCCU, thousands of ethnic minority faculty, students, and staff (modern-day Hellenistic Jews) are raising their voices in prophetic complaint against the perceived hoarding of educational resources and opportunities by white administrative leaders (modern-day Hebraic Jews) who control the resources of their institutions. The approach taken by the senior leader in my counterstory began in the commendable example of Acts 6 but then reversed course.

As Hebraic Jews and the first leaders of the primitive church, the Twelve listened to the complaints that were presented to them by their Hellenistic cousins. According to the account we have in Acts 6, their first response was not defensiveness. They did not deny and deflect the complaints, as is so often the case when cultural critique is raised today in the context of the local church or Christian colleges and seminaries. They did not reply with an ancient version of reactionary color blindness that said, "You're taking it the wrong way. We don't see a difference between Hebrew and Greek widows. We haven't spoken any explicit words of hostility against you, nor did ethnicity have anything to do with our distribution practices. You're making much ado about nothing. We're all just children of Abraham." Instead, they trusted and shifted power to their Greek cousins in order

41. Jennings, *Acts*, 65.

to find a solution to the problem.[42] Believing that the Holy Spirit was equally at work in the lives and hearts of their diaspora siblings, they called all the disciples together and appointed Greek stakeholders to create a new structure that would ensure equitable distribution of resources to Hebrew and Greek widows alike. Scholars think that these first "deacons" were most likely immigrants to Jerusalem from the diaspora because of their Greek names. Indeed, the final deacon mentioned—Nicolas from Antioch—was even a gentile convert to Judaism and the way of Jesus. We are told that the result of such power sharing with Hellenistic leaders was that "the word of God spread. The number of disciples in Jerusalem increased rapidly, and a large number of priests became obedient to the faith" (Acts 6:7).

In the case of my experience at the Christian university, the senior executive leadership initially followed the example of Acts 6 by appointing a search committee that was diverse in both gender and ethnicity. When the final decision was made, however, the provost chose to act unilaterally. When push came to shove, he did not really trust the perspectives and leadership of the modern-day "Hellenistic" sisters and brothers of his campus. In the language of CRT, he did not embrace the voice of color thesis. He did not trust that the diverse leaders of color that were appointed for the task, who were "known to be full of the Spirit and wisdom," were best equipped to understand and solve the very racial problems on campus that they directly experienced.

The provost's actions would have been equivalent to the Twelve appointing the first group of Greek deacons to solve the problem of inequitable distribution but then disbanding them and rejecting their recommendations. Unfortunately,

42. Salvatierra and Wrencher, *Buried Seeds*.

this pattern is replicated many times throughout the United States in local churches, denominations, CCCU institutions, campus ministries, and elsewhere. We ethnic minorities are told that our perspectives and leadership gifts matter, but in the end we remain tokenized, and power remains in the hands of white leaders who retain the racial and cultural status quo.

## Conclusion: Voices of Hope

Utilizing the CRT tools of the voice of color thesis and critical race counterstories—together with their biblical corollaries—this chapter has explored some of the creative work being done to reform theological education in the United States and has examined several of the major structural roadblocks hampering the effective diversification of Christian higher education. I have argued that an unbiblical expression of color blindness is chief among these obstacles. This reactionary color blindness lacks a biblical understanding of the positive contributions of cultural diversity as represented by John the Seer in the book of Revelation as the "glory and honor of the nations." As a consequence, those possessing a philosophical precommitment to color blindness find little problem with the lack of cultural diversity that characterizes leadership in Christian higher education and may even oppose urgent and proactive measures to diversify their institutions. They are quite literally "blind" to the profound value of the cultural treasure and community cultural wealth embodied by the diverse community of people that the Holy Spirit of God is assembling in the United States as a dress rehearsal for the New Jerusalem. In order to keep step with the Spirit, revitalization of our seminaries and Christian colleges and universities requires curricular and structural overhaul that takes seriously the theological principle of the "glory and honor of the nations" and the biblical vision of people from every tribe, language, nation, and tongue playing their distinct roles of leadership in the body of Christ.

But as I have learned from my coauthor, a valid criticism of CRT is that, though it offers effective tools for smoking out racism in structures and institutions, it does not offer a larger eschatological hope for change. Seeing and analyzing all the systemic racism that lingers in our churches and religious institutions can easily cause one to become trapped in despair or locked into cynicism. As a follower of Jesus and a CRT practitioner, I do not wish to end this chapter by making this mistake.

As students and apprentices of Jesus, we possess a unique hope. Though oftentimes those of us engaged in the work of racial justice in Christian institutions may feel hard pressed, perplexed, and even persecuted, may we keep our eyes on Jesus and be reminded that, like in the prophets of old, his life is also revealed in us. God has not stopped renewing the church by the Spirit.[43] The Spirit is moving us toward the final eschatological goal of the beloved community composed of people of every nation, language, tribe, and tongue. And by the grace of God, we are instruments of God's beloved community.

> After this I looked, and there before me was a great multitude that no one could count, from every nation, tribe, people and language, standing before the throne and before the Lamb. They were wearing white robes and were holding palm branches in their hands. And they cried out in a loud voice:

43. Yong, *Renewing the Church*.

"Salvation belongs to our God,
who sits on the throne,
and to the Lamb."

Revelation 7:9–10

We find hope not just because we know how the story of history will end but also because of the testimony of those who have gone before us. Just as the earliest Christians insisted that Jesus was Lord and Savior—despite their insignificant numbers and the crushing weight of Roman imperialism and persecution—and continued to believe and embody the truth that Jesus inaugurated a loving kingdom that would transform all of us and all things, so must we as justice-minded Christians never lose sight of this same hope. As reflected in the critical race counterstories shared in this chapter, this work of biblical diversity, equity, and inclusion in Christian higher education is often challenging and lonely. Like the seven churches of the book of Revelation, it brings us literally and figuratively into direct confrontation with the beasts, systems, structures, and ideologies that have buttressed five centuries of empire in the Americas. It is a spiritual battle. It is a war.

Like the early church, however, may we overcome "by the blood of the Lamb and by the word of [our] testimony" (Rev. 12:11). And in our most difficult moments, may we be reminded that "we have this treasure in jars of clay to show that this all-surpassing power is from God and not from us. We are hard pressed on every side, but not crushed; perplexed, but not in despair; persecuted, but not abandoned; struck down, but not destroyed. We always carry around in our body the death of Jesus, so that the life of Jesus may also be revealed in our body" (2 Cor. 4:7–10).

I am encouraged not only by the witness of Scripture and of the historic church but also by the fact that God has currently raised up many diverse leaders in Christian colleges, universities, and seminaries throughout the country who share this biblical vision and who are spearheading change, day by day, in the trenches of Christian academia. Some are personal friends; some I have respected and admired from afar; all are sisters and brothers. Here are but a few: Elizabeth Conde-Frazier, Edwin Aponte, Michelle Loyd-Paige, Willie Jennings, Amos Yong, Mark Labberton, Joanne Rodríguez, Marty Harris, Daisy Machado, Lucila Crena, D. A. Horton, Pete Menjares, Aaron Hinojosa, Glen Kinoshita, Karen Longman, Andrea Scott, Alexander Jun, Love Sechrest, Johnny Ramírez-Johnson, Allison Ash, Luis R. Rivera, Alexia Salvatierra, Juan Martinez, Justo González, Rebecca Torres Valdovinos, Fernando Cascante, Karen Figueroa, Eliezer Álvarez-Diaz, Michael Emerson, Daniel Lee, Janette Hur Ok, Kay Higuera Smith, Andrea Cook, Vince Bantu, Raymond Chang, Rukshan Fernando, Leah Fulton, Felix Muniz, Kimberly Battle-Walters Denu, Edwin Estevez, Jeanette Hsieh, Jenny Elsey, Nathan Cartagena, Shirley Hoogstra, John Witvliet, David Bailey, Octavio Esqueda, Oscar García-Johnson, Kathy-Ann Hernandez, Rebecca Hernandez, Antonio Mejico Jr., Charles Lee-Johnson, and Joanne Solis-Walker. Drawing from the authority of Scripture, and sometimes from the language of CRT and other theoretical frameworks that might be helpful in capturing their God-directed experiences in Christian higher education, these leaders are on the leading edge of articulating the deep racial concerns that continue to impact the nation and Christian educational institutions. And they do so with a deep commitment to Christ, his church, and the project of God's shalom in the world. Many of their experiences, challenges, and insights have been articulated in peer-reviewed journal articles, books, and essay collections.[44]

As they move forward in God's sacred calling, these individuals, along with many others, have created various centers, institutes, conferences, and initiatives to promote the cause of equity and diversity. The Association for Hispanic Theological Education, the Hispanic Theological Initiative, the Hispanic Summer Program, and the Galilean Theological Center have already been discussed. Some others include the CCCU's Multi-ethnic Leadership Development Institute; the Student Congress on Racial Reconciliation; the Justo and Catherine González Resource Center; the Jesse Miranda Center for Hispanic Leadership and the Global Center for Women and Justice at Vanguard University; the Hispanic Center for Theological Studies; the Center for Justice and Reconciliation at Point Loma Nazarene University; the John Perkins Center at Seattle Pacific University; and Fuller Theological Seminary's Centro Latino, William E. Pannell Center for Black Church Studies, Center for Asian American Theology and Ministry, Korean Studies Center, and Chinese Studies Center. The many who serve as chief diversity officers and multicultural affairs staff across the CCCU also deserve recognition for their tireless efforts.

As stated by college president, pastor, and education scholar Pete Menjares, the faculty, staff, and administrators who support these various biblical diversity projects interpret the current influx of diverse students across the CCCU as a "'Kairos moment' . . . a time when God is moving

44. Here are just a few examples: Loyd-Paige and Williams, *Diversity Playbook*; Longman, *Diversity Matters*; Conde-Frazier, *Atando Cabos*; Jennings, *After Whiteness*; Yong, *Renewing the Church*; Jun et al., *White Jesus*; Sun, *Attempt Great Things for God*; and Pazmiño and Esqueda, *Anointed Teaching*.

significantly in human history."[45] With prophetic wisdom and grace, Menjares and others are working diligently to comprehensively reimagine Christian higher education in a way that embodies the diversity of the kingdom of God in its student body, faculty, staff, and senior leadership, and that "keep[s] in step with the 'new thing' God is doing at present."[46] I join them. They give me hope.

45. Menjares, "Diversity in the CCCU," 14.
46. Menjares, "Diversity in the CCCU," 14.

# 4

# Consummation

## The Beloved Community

### Introduction

In the early 2010s, I (Jeff) traveled with a group of seminary faculty and PhD students to a country with two Christian movements: one that was sanctioned by the state and one that was not. One evening, our delegation enjoyed an impressive reception banquet with a government-registered group of clergy from a particular locale. Not every member of our group spoke the language, but none of us could miss the intensity that was beginning to rise. One of the clergy, with eyes tearing up, voice quavering, and finger pointing accusingly, asked why Western Christians primarily concerned themselves with and advocated for the *non*sanctioned Christian movement. After all, he protested, when officials came knocking on his door, searching for nonsanctioned clergy and their parishioners, it was he who covered for them at great risk to himself and for the sake of the body of Christ. I could scarcely take another bite, as this man's painful desolation began to stick in my throat.

My own formation has largely taken place among Christians whose political theology reflects a cruel irony. We have imagined ourselves as the legacies of faithfulness-amid-persecution contiguous with the biblical exodus narrative. This mythos causes us to invest our sympathies and our financial resources toward the global Christian movements in which we see our mythical selves reflected. In many of our Western, democratic minds, the country's state-sanctioned Christian movement could only ever be theologically compromised by statist loyalties. This deficit thinking has led to a kind of disownment and disavowal of members of the body of Christ. Ranging from the million paper cuts of going unheard, to being accosted by white nationalist trolls, to having our Christian confession rejected, these forms of disownment and disavowal misshape all parties involved. The irony, of course, is that my own Christian community has been possessed *by* its investment in political power and influence, wielding it in ways that serve its interests to further establish and legitimate the present order of things. We do this all while viewing ourselves as misfortunate targets of creeping secularity, moral chaos, and all sorts of phenomena that threaten the story we tell ourselves. In a chapter on community, the first-person plural here is deliberate. These are my people.

To feel alienated from one's spiritual community by disownment and disavowal is deeply painful. This pertains to the growing number of people who are committed to racial justice and view it as inseparable from their understanding of the mission of God in the world and yet face ideological skepticism, microaggressions, and discriminatory conduct in their churches and organizations. These spaces have become toxic and untenable, responsible, in part, for mass disaffiliation. Many who have left their churches are now ecclesially adrift, wondering if there are communities of belonging available to them at all. Additionally, it is a strong temptation to return disavowal for disavowal, indulging a vicious cycle of psychic retaliation that, in my pastoral experience, leads not to liberation but to perpetual hauntedness. Despite the usefulness of CRT, and though the charge of "divisiveness" against CRT is deliberately and deceitfully overblown, I turn back to the previous chapter's concluding note of hope in the beloved community.

Let me first illustrate what is intended by the oft-used phrase *beloved community*. In my second year of working as a resident adviser for the University of Michigan, having informed my supervisors, I made the difficult choice to break the rules and leave a training event where all the student employees were simulating a "living and learning community." This training event spanned a Sunday, and my commitment to worshiping with my ecclesial family at Knox Presbyterian Church was nonnegotiable. When I returned from church that Sunday, I opened my door to find a termination letter. I was fired, effective immediately. A fellow second-year adviser took up my cause. He and I had had countless conversations during the prior year. We had talked about Edward Said's notion of orientalism, the Palestinian cause, race, Christianity, and justice. Across race and religion, we shared a common vision of serving students and an experience of religious primacy. I would hear later that he led our fellow resident advisers in a protest, chanting for my reinstatement—which I received only a few days later. His moral clarity, friendship, and solidarity were beyond surprising and honoring to me. He made my problems his problems for righteousness's sake. This was one of my earliest tastes of beloved community.

## Theology for Beloved Community

The Rev. Dr. Martin Luther King Jr. popularized the term *beloved community* during the civil rights movement. King repeatedly marveled at his experience of the Montgomery bus boycott. Of course, the boycott was a watershed moment, but King would be clear that a strategic victory for and demonstration of the power of nonviolence, however significant, was not the end goal. Rather, he would reiterate that "noncooperation and boycotts are not ends themselves; they are merely means to awaken a sense of moral shame in the opponent. The end is redemption and reconciliation. The aftermath of nonviolence is the creation of the beloved community."[1] King never produced a systematic theology, but his sermons and speeches demonstrate his extensive theological training, his pastoral calling, and his Christian confession, which fill the beloved community with sublime connotation.

The idea of beloved community, therefore, cannot be evacuated of its theological content without doing significant damage. Works that treat the beloved community as little more than an inclusive or diverse community miss its theological and missional significance. The beloved community is not a mere concept or abstract aspiration. Civil rights historian Ralph Luker traced the development of King's use of the phrase. His earliest uses coincided with strategic wins in Montgomery—a hope emerging from real phenomena.

1. King, "Nonviolence and Racial Justice," 166.

Furthermore, Luker writes, "King was elated to find that divisions of religious denomination and social class were eroded and miracles of self transformation occurred as ordinary people translated accumulated resentments from sullen acquiescence into determined courage."[2] King's own surprise at ecumenical and interfaith co-belligerence and real, personal, moral transformation would alter his understanding of his work, just as the disruptive influx of gentiles into the family of God irreversibly altered the character of early Christian mission. Luker views this as a kind of intermediate space "beyond church, but short of the Kingdom."[3]

This intermediate space is not far from what theologians call "inaugurated eschatology." At its most basic, inaugurated eschatology is what gives Christians the language of "already, not yet." In the cross and resurrection, the power of God has *already* broken into the world, and Christians enjoy the hopeful promise of resurrection power in this life. Temporally, however, the end of all things is *not yet*. Christian communities and justice movements alike exist in this in-between time. Considering this liminality, Charles Marsh writes,

> The beloved community may then finally be described as a gift of the kingdom of God introduced into history by the church, and thus it exists within the provenance of Christ's mystery in the world. When the beloved community remembers the gift, its witness is strengthened as its energy for service is renewed; when it celebrates the gift in praise and proclamation, the beloved community exists as the church, which it has always been in its essence. One could say that the relationship between church and beloved community is

2. Luker, "Kingdom of God," 43.
3. Luker, "Kingdom of God," 44.

mutually enriching, even as the church remains at all times theologically prior. In other words, the church establishes the hidden meaning of beloved community even as beloved community makes visible that meaning in ways the church may often not.[4]

Several elements are important here. First, the implications for theological method become concrete in the beloved community. Rather than abstract, unknown, and unknowable time—however immanent—the beloved community, like the church, comprises human bodies in real time and space, in relation to one another, for a shared purpose. Second, the love and justice that characterize beloved community are not always embodied in the church. In fact, in this fraught time, and in the contentious debate over CRT, churches and movements are tragically branded by their contempt and against-ness instead of being known for their love of God and neighbor. Third, and most importantly, Marsh has rightly understood that spiritual power—in particular, the spiritual power promised to the people of God—is part and parcel of what King imagines in beloved community.

That King holds together direct action and personal transformation is no less significant. In so much evangelical eschatology, individualistic concern about personal preparedness for deliverance from tribulation overshadows the gloriousness of Christ's return and its implication for the cosmos. The ethical implications of an eschatology that envisions a complete disruption with the present time disincentivizes social action by making ethical outcomes irrelevant in comparison to a preferential option for the sweet by-and-by. To the contrary, Derek Hicks's account of African American

4. Marsh, *Beloved Community*, 207.

eschatology foregrounds the importance of black experience and ethics in theology:

> Evangelical constructions of eschatology give an account of God's program in the biblical-supernatural-heavenly-eternal spheres in connection to personal faith and piety. But an eschatology based in individual rewards falls flat for African Americans, many of whom seek answers that explain why other Christians have for so long challenged their humanity. They seek a community-based eschatology. African American theology critiques evangelical eschatology for its failure to capture the existential plight of believers as well. For it, African American theology, eschatological analysis must also be grounded in the historical present, and must challenge present circumstances that stand in contrast to God's desire for justice and equality for all people.[5]

Similarly, Loida Martell-Otero writes, "From an evangélica perspective, I argue that eschatology is about the fulfillment of God's vision—one that began at creation. This vision is related to the holistic formation of community and responds to God's command for justice and mercy."[6] When theological method resists reflection on the experiences of people of color and eschews concrete work toward racial justice, that resistance resonates with anti-CRT pundits who attempt to argue that CRT prefers "experience" in epistemology to "science." In an idealist frame, Christian "worldview" language challenges narratives of experience in preference to "truth."

It is important to pause here to acknowledge a significant difference between CRT and Christian theology. In a section

5. Hicks, "Eschatology in African American Theology," 251.

6. Martell-Otero, Maldonado Pérez, and Conde-Frazier, *Latina Evangélicas*, 109.

that illustrates critical race theorists' engagement with critiques against it, Richard Delgado and Jean Stefancic have written briefly and frankly about their view of claims to objectivity: "For the critical race theorist, objective truth, like merit, does not exist, at least in social science and politics. In these realms, truth is a social construct created to suit the purposes of the dominant group."[7] On the one hand, this suspicious hermeneutic is what makes CRT so useful in examining the ways that dominance and power bend ideas, structures, and policies to benefit the strong. As of the writing of this chapter, serious and horrific abuses of power have made the headlines, further eroding the credibility of clergy in the United States, causing many to call into question the theologies and doctrines that established and sustained such harmful people and organizations.[8] On the other hand, creedal Christians do not all share this suspicion of the commitments by which we live into the Christian story. For example, I confess along with others that "the church receives and approves" the Bible as "holy and canonical, for the regulating, founding, and establishing of our faith."[9]

Furthermore, legal scholar Brandon Paradise observes that CRT has, for the most part, neglected what he calls the "normative resources of the African American Christian tradition."[10] Paradise explains the following: "CRT seems to

7. Delgado and Stefancic, *Critical Race Theory*, 104.

8. "Pastors' Credibility Is in Question—Even among Pastors," Barna, February 16, 2022, https://www.barna.com/research/pastors-trustworthy-reliable/?fbclid=IwAR1NytNUz8Hdu5UXnf1vK48CBh0VT_QgY_P_p9qwi-R5zIu8TXPuavE8qSw.

9. "Article 5: The Authority of Scripture," Belgic Confession, Christian Reformed Church, accessed April 15, 2022, https://www.crcna.org/welcome/beliefs/confessions/belgic-confession#toc-article-5-the-authority-of-scripture.

10. Paradise argues that post-structuralist approaches to antidiscrimination and to the explanation of human culture are thoroughly incongruous with, for example, theological anthropology. He draws on a view of human selfhood as

view domination and subordination exclusively as the product of power relations constructed by human beings, and therefore proceeds along a naturalistic theoretical framework that cannot easily accommodate the classical Christian notion that spiritual imperfections limit humanity's capacity to build domination-free social structures. In addition, and consistent with this naturalistic framework, according to the internal logic of CRT's constructionist antisubordination principle, religion is a social factor, that, like all social factors, should be critiqued from an antisubordination perspective."[11]

While there are notable exceptions to this general observation,[12] this lacuna is not a surprise, but neither is it prohibitive to substantive theological engagement going forward—as we have sought to demonstrate. Rather, it is more likely worldview*ism* that places nonconstructive limits on engagement with the academic disciplines—including CRT—and forecloses possibilities for beloved community.

## Christ, Culture, and Beloved Community

I was a college student when I became interested in Christian thought. I had previously begun asking classic apologetics questions in high school and later leaned into reading apologetics texts and blogs—often instead of faithfully studying my major. My mind felt alive when exploring new vistas and possibilities, which I then tested out on roommates, labmates, and friends. I was excited that my "worldview," as the

constituted by "language games" in contrast to the African American Christian resource of the doctrine of the image of God, in which dignity and worth are inherent to humans by virtue of our creatureliness. Paradise, "How Critical Race Theory Marginalizes," 129.

11. Paradise, "How Critical Race Theory Marginalizes," 168.

12. Paradise rightly recalls Anthony Cook's 1990 article in the *Harvard Law Review*, "Beyond Critical Legal Studies."

apologists called it, might be a transmissible body of knowledge. Also enticing was the idea propounded by Reformed apologetics that only the Christian worldview could account for rationality and possessed internal consistency. On the whole, if I honed my skill, deepened my thought life, and was persuasive and winsome, then I would earn, at the very least, the respect of skeptics. The best I might do is convince someone to consider Jesus with openness to faith. I invested heavily in this intellectual and theological formation. In fact, if I overslept on a Sunday morning, I believed I could turn to an online lecture archive for a meaningful substitute! My grasp of both apologetics and its formational influence were rudimentary, naive, and filled with unconscious ambition. At my best, however, I leaned into apologetics for the sake of evangelistic mission among beloved friends for whom I cared deeply.

In fact, I believe it was this core desire that propelled me to become a university chaplain. I was excited to work at a consortium of colleges in Southern California that was known for its progressive faculty and student body. To illustrate the ideological environment, Pomona College, one of the member schools in the consortium, reports that a meager 3 percent of its student body identifies as politically conservative, while 77 percent describe themselves as liberal or very liberal.[13] The numbers are similar for faculty. This alone was appealing to me as I framed ideological polarization as the cultural challenge for which I underwent so much cross-cultural ministry training. The unexpected blessing of working at the Claremont Colleges was the beloved community I experienced in interfaith work. We did not walk

---

13. "Perceptions of Speech and Campus Climate: 2018 Gallup Survey of Pomona Students and Faculty," Pomona College, accessed December 11, 2021, https://www.pomona.edu/public-dialogue/survey.

into any bars together, but our interfaith center's staff was the start of a classic joke—a rabbi, an imam, a priest, and a pastor (me). Our work with religious, spiritual, and nonreligious/spiritual students afforded us numerous opportunities to behold one another's humanity, traditions, rituals, hopes, and dreams. We also had the opportunity to care for the student body when tragedy struck.

So far, I have focused in this chapter on Christian community and its overlap with the beloved community. King, however, in referring to beloved community, did not limit the work of racial justice to church folk. His meaningful learning from Mahatma Gandhi, his partnership with Rabbi Abraham Joshua Heschel in Montgomery, and his friendship with Buddhist monk Thich Nhat Hanh all informed the scope of what he meant by *beloved community*.

As a young student of apologetics who was leaning into worldviewism, I could not have imagined the interfaith community I would come to experience at Claremont. I had been invested in dissecting and critiquing other religious worldviews in order to advance mine. Tacitly, I had learned to imagine Christianity as the rightfully regnant worldview in the United States, along with all the theopolitical ramifications. All the while, my ministry experience was telling me something that I had been resisting—namely, that Charles Taylor's "secular age" was a more apt characterization of the pluralistic world in which we live.[14] For the purposes of this chapter, I simply intend to call to mind Taylor's description of our times—namely, times in which spirituality in general (and Christianity in particular) is one of many options. My worldviewism caused me to think and act to the contrary. I could learn only the most token and impractical lessons from

14. Taylor, *Secular Age*.

other traditions, and all of them were in need of my correction. My engagement with culture took an oppositional posture that could fairly be considered "Constantinian," in the sense that it was blind to and presumptuous of its own dominance. The modes of campus ministry associated with this posture displayed neglect of the formative power of the academic disciplines in the lives of students. I found myself teaching *via negativa* by emphasizing the views that my worldview rejected—sometimes even more than I taught the convictions that I affirmed. Ministry was characterized by, among other things, disavowal and disownment. It also led me to view faculty as distracted (and distracting students) from what I unconsciously considered to be higher, "spiritual" priorities—as if the Spirit of God did not indwell faculty or direct their work as they studied and loved the world God has made.

I recognize this posture in so many truly well-intentioned Christians. When I announced that I would become the interfaith Protestant chaplain, many church members expressed their intentions to support me in prayer because the campus could be a "dark place," "very liberal," and so on. I also recall a student affairs representative for a Christian college telling parents of prospective students that one central reason to consider Christian higher education is faith retention. In other words, the university is often feared as a place where our children's spirituality goes to die. This fearful and oppositional posture toward such a significant driver of wider culture is not new. For example, Christians grappled with the discipline of psychology in the 1940s and 1950s. Some found psychology's secularity too problematic, and the Christian alternative to psychotherapy, called "biblical counseling," emerged in the 1970s. Others would work on theologically informed approaches to "integration." One's posture toward

CRT, too, falls into the long-standing "Christ and culture" conversation.[15]

Ultimately, an oppositional posture causes mutual suspicion to spiral out of control and makes beloved community impossible apart from reorientation. As Richard Mouw observes, "For Reformed Christians who take seriously the reality of the antithesis between belief and unbelief, the theological rationale for positive and holy feelings toward the larger human community does not come easily."[16] Mouw's discussion of the emphasis on antithesis both in the Dutch Reformed theology of Klaas Schilder and in Anabaptist theology suggests that there are many reasons (some more carefully crafted than others) for hesitancy when engaging the world of ideas that includes CRT. However, Mouw also gleans from Schilder that car*ing* (not just care*ful*) attention to the significant rupture between belief and unbelief is necessary for faithful witness. Looking toward the end-times, in which Christians will face the threat of an Antichrist, Mouw writes that we learn to resist the deceit and power of evil "by looking for special signs of lawlessness, of rebellion—overt or subtle—against God's creating and redeeming purposes in the world. These signs include the broader patterns of lawlessness that show a disregard for that which God deeply cares about: racial justice, the plight of the poor, fidelity in human relationships, the dignity of the nonhuman created order. As long as we prepare ourselves to oppose this lawlessness wherever and whenever it appears, a sensitivity

---

15. Many will be familiar with H. Richard Niebuhr's 1951 book, *Christ and Culture*. Since then, many theologians and biblical scholars have reflected on Niebuhr's groundbreaking work. This chapter reflects the influence of critiques that point out the ways in which Niebuhr's theological imagination presupposes the dominance of the Christian tradition and a culture-transforming imperative for Christians. See, for example, C. Carter, *Rethinking Christ and Culture*.

16. Mouw, *Challenges of Cultural Discipleship*, 144.

to warnings about the future can serve to strengthen us for faithfulness to the gospel."[17]

Surprisingly, it is Christian reflection on the antithesis that reorients us to beloved community with those who are engaged in the work of racial justice, opening the possibility of a shared telos. This is what it can mean to oppose racism in all its forms: that the well-formed Christian imagination is able to identify the signs of eschatological lawlessness, to articulate and reject the conditions from which it arises, to announce a gospel-shaped counterstory, and to welcome the disruption of beloved community as an inbreaking (however incomplete) of the righteousness and justice to come. Even Paradise's critique of CRT is suggestive of ways in which the normative resources of the African American Christian tradition, such as the image of God and ethics associated with *agapē*, are antithetical to CRT's philosophical assumptions *while* they envision the shared goal of antisubordination.

If it is possible for Christian reflection on the antithesis to yield this reorientation, then it must be said that neglect of such reflection can lead to premature, wholesale rejection or adoption of an academic movement like CRT. If, however, the beloved community is "beyond church, but short of the Kingdom," one's approach to Christ and culture functions as a discernment of the Spirit's activity that energizes the beloved community. Rather than seeing the world outside the hard boundaries of the Christian community as bereft of the goodness of God (a form of deficit thinking), the beloved community responds "to what is good, and to God's call through this."[18] William Dyrness proposes a *theologia poetica* that invites Christians to go beyond understanding cultural phenomena (namely, worldviewism) to offering a

17. Mouw, *Challenges of Cultural Discipleship*, 138.
18. Dyrness, *Poetic Theology*, 81.

full response to God's presence in culture that involves intellect, desires, and emotions. For Dyrness, culture and human participation in culture-making are theological sites where people can seek after God. I join with other theologians, Christian scholars, and activists who are learning that wherever justice and dignity are being secured for those to whom it has been denied, that is where God is working.

## CRT's Gloomy Eschaton

Sadly, I do not expect critical race theorists to join me in the kind of eschatological hope that is rooted in the normative resources of the Christian tradition. CRT's outlook on the future can be bleak. This is not merely a Niebuhrian type of realism that articulates the harsh reality about the pervasiveness of sin and its effects. While there are those who speculate about a future in which CRT may become the new orthodoxy (e.g., Delgado and Stefancic), there are others who expect far worse outcomes. Derrick Bell writes the following: "It is time we concede that a commitment to racial equality merely perpetuates our disempowerment. Rather, we need a mechanism to make life bearable in a society where blacks are a permanent, subordinate class. Our empowerment lies in recognizing that Racial Realism may open the gateway to attaining a more meaningful status."[19]

In his frequently cited article, Bell takes aim at "legal formalism." In the footnotes, Bell cites Judge Richard Posner's treatment of legal formalism, which Posner defines as "the use of deductive logic to derive the outcome of a case from premises accepted as authoritative."[20] Bell, however, believes

19. Bell, "Racial Realism," 377.
20. Posner, "Legal Formalism," 181. In my view, there is a resonance between this approach to jurisprudence and the use of worldview. The legal premises that,

that formalism can diminish a value like "equality" by relegating it to the realm of abstract ideas and neglecting the functions of law that either do or do not make equality a reality. It is important, additionally, to give the bleak notion of permanent subordinate status a full hearing. Bell explains that confidence is misplaced in abstract notions of racial equality that are impossible to realize, secure, or guarantee, saying that judges "may advocate the importance of racial equality while arriving at a decision detrimental to black Americans."[21] According to Lani Guinier and Gerald Torres, "Even when legal rights grant those with a grievance a highly individualistic remedy, the definition of those rights can be manipulated over time by clever lawyers and conservative judges to legitimate the status quo."[22] In other words, functionally nullifying civil rights gains may not always be the action of a single judge but can be the product of the logic of those who are invested in business as usual. So to misplace one's trust in the promise of an "equality" that will never be realized is, for Bell and others, not hopeful at all.[23]

Hence, critical race theorists call for a different investment of activist energy. Bell's article ends with his recollection of

for example, originalist interpreters of the constitution hold to be authoritative are not unlike the premises about rationality and authoritative doctrinal premises in theology. In both cases, questioning these premises quickly generates significant heat.

21. Bell, "Racial Realism," 376.

22. Guinier and Torres, "Changing the Wind."

23. However, to the extent that Christian theology neglects its own functional and practical aspects, the promises of "equality at the foot of the cross" (to borrow a popular phrase) can also be too abstract. In fact, the inscrutable timing of the parousia itself creates both abstractness and an ethical disjunct that some Christians use to absolve themselves from faithful action on the "already" side of heaven. In other words, the problems that attend abstraction are not legal formalism's alone. Additionally, see Jonathan Tran's thoughtful treatment of Afropessimism—a critical framework somewhat adjacent to that of theorists like Derrick Bell and Cornel West. In his transition from exposition to critical analysis of Afropessimism, Tran rehearses a majestic eschatological vision. Tran, *Asian Americans and the Spirit of Racial Capitalism*, 274–87.

his interview with a civil rights worker by the name of Biona MacDonald in 1964. When Bell asked her about her motivation to face hostile conditions in her work, she replied, "I am an old woman. I lives to harass white folk." Bell reflects on this pithy reply with pastoral insight:

> Mrs. MacDonald did not even hint that her harassment would topple whites' well-entrenched power. Rather, her goal was defiance and its harassing effect was more potent precisely because she placed herself in confrontation with her oppressors with full knowledge of their power and willingness to use it.
>
> Mrs. MacDonald avoided discouragement and defeat because at the point that she determined to resist her oppression, she was triumphant. Nothing the all-powerful whites could do to her would diminish her triumph. Mrs. MacDonald understood twenty-five years ago the theory that I am espousing in the 1990s for black leaders and civil rights lawyers to adopt. If you remember her story, you will understand my message.[24]

Though I am cautious and wish to avoid overprescribing, I read in CRT the conviction that resistance to oppression in the face of impossible odds is dignified and ennobling in its own way.[25] Furthermore, to behold activist energy among those who understand themselves as facing such odds is an opportunity for onlookers to identify the deeply human yearning for dignity and freedom. So as critical race theorists listen to activists working for better conditions, they develop theories and critiques that assist activists in challenging the systems and structures that give rise to unjust conditions.

24. Bell, "Racial Realism," 379.
25. Drawing from the theology and ethics of Rev. Dr. Martin Luther King Jr., I find this to be particularly true of nonviolent direct action.

That is to say, the goal of their theorizing is a *vision* of a different social order.[26]

There are, however, reasons to attenuate enthusiasm for Bell's advice to racialized and marginalized groups. From within CRT, Berkeley law professor John Powell makes central the role of struggle against power precisely because the real effects of racial inequality ravage black communities. Powell argues, "The idealism of Racial Realism suggests that if we free ourselves from the false theory of equality, we will not suffer from despair—even though our children will continue to die from disease or gun play, and our lives will continue to be circumscribed by white domination."[27] Powell sustains Bell's objection to the abstractness of "formal equality" that dominates jurisprudence in the United States. However, Powell argues in a later work that "we must acknowledge that subordination affects the position of both the dominant and the dominated."[28] This expression of the simultaneous mis-shaping of dominant and dominated can also be found in the Kingian understanding of one of the Bible's words for love: *agapē*. The dehumanization that oppressed peoples suffer cannot be separated from the disfigurement of the perpetrators of racism. Hence, the kind of "creative suffering" that King orchestrated and applauded is better funded by the power of *agapē*, and both Powell's and King's visions require a transformational confrontation with white supremacy in society rather than mere disavowal and disownment of

26. Whether activists on the ground share or take up that vision is another matter. In fact, Paradise points to the work of black church scholars Eric Lincoln and Lawrence Mamiya, who observe the relatively slow spread of black liberation theology among black clergy. They specifically name the "middle-class origins" of black liberation theology as an ironic contrast and a hurdle to its aims of doing theology from below. Lincoln and Mamiya, *Black Church*, 180.

27. Powell, "Racial Realism or Racial Despair," 545.

28. Powell, *Racing to Justice*, 194.

oppressive systems and structures in society. On the way to CRT's preferred future, CRT does not guarantee the psychic welfare of the communities it hopes to serve, nor does its emphasis on systems and structures take seriously the personal, moral transformation (vis-à-vis Dr. King's emphasis here) of people who benefit from the present order.

## CRT and the Discourse of Death

My concern about CRT's gloomy eschaton is that it can serve as backward justification for an ethic of disavowal and disownment that ensconces one in a cycle of rhetorical violence. At the risk of sounding dramatic, I have called it a "discourse of death."[29] Dutch Catholic priest Henri Nouwen reflected on his conversations with activists who worked against nuclear proliferation and detected in their discourse a thread that is woven through common, nonactivist parlance too.

> Many peacemakers, overwhelmed by the great threats of our time, have lost their joy and have become prophets of doom. Yet anyone who grimly announces the end of the world and then hopes to move people to peace work is not a peacemaker. Peace and joy are like brother and sister; they belong together. I cannot remember a moment of peace in my life that wasn't also very joyful. In the Gospels, joy and peace are always found together. . . . The Gospel of peace is also a Gospel of joy. Thus, peace work is joyful work.[30]

Along with others, I do not always feel joy when working for racial justice. Emerging clinical descriptions of "racial

29. Jeff Liou, "Disownment and the Discourse of Death," *The Politics of Scripture* (blog), Political Theology Network, September 13, 2021, https://political theology.com/disownment-and-the-discourse-of-death/.

30. Nouwen, *Peacework*, 56–57.

trauma" and "moral injury" give new vocabulary and texture to the manifold ways in which people of color experience the world around them.

In 2019, I was notified that an elderly Asian American woman in our congregation had been brutally murdered. Though I was no longer on the staff of the church where this "auntie" and I worshiped, I knew that culturally informed care was in short supply, so I engaged the weighty privilege of providing pastoral care and funerary services for the surviving family. It may be hard or impossible for readers to enter into my experience, but in watching this family grieve, I could not help but see the racialized bodies of *all* my Asian American "aunties" and "uncles" as vulnerable. To my horror, since March 2020 more than ten thousand hate incidents have been reported to the organization Stop AAPI Hate.[31] Asian Americans, especially women and the elderly, have been the targets of heinous acts of violence. Local churches' effete responses have been injurious, and sometimes that wounding accrues to Asian American congregants unawares. I have simply not been able to consider the enduring racist mistreatment from congregation members and the silence of the clergy charged with our care as "joyful"—but that is not what Nouwen is prescribing.

I am instead attempting to identify the gravitational pull of the discourse of death. The discourse of death is less about the "critical" or "revolutionary" spirit by which some Christian leaders feel threatened. Certainly the phrase *discourse of death* is not intended to disparage the legitimate, prophetic rage marginalized people feel.[32] Rather, I am concerned about the ravages of desolation made manifest in

---

31. "National Report (through December 31, 2021)," Stop AAPI Hate, https://stopaapihate.org/national-report-through-december-31-2021/.

32. See Hill, *Prophetic Rage*.

violence of spirit. Martin Luther King's characterization of the activists in the Montgomery Improvement Association, and of nonviolent resistance generally, includes "refraining from not only physical violence but also from violence of spirit."[33] As has already been made clear, King's tactics were not the end; beloved community free from such violence was. CRT may deliberately and methodologically reject the kind of personal transformations, spiritual and moral, that are normative in the African American Christian tradition. White evangelicalism may be unable to imagine spiritual transformation that inclines us to the material exigencies that communities of color experience. The beloved community that King imagined assumes it, while the discourse of death dismisses it. Neglecting spiritual deliverance from the principality of violence will do nothing to curtail endless cycles of disownment and alienation, and any fundamentalist idealogue (be they conservative or progressive, identarian or color-blind) will be capable of dragging others with them into the discourse of death.

Thankfully, there are lessons to be learned from discourse in Scripture. Consider, for example, James's letter to the Jewish Christian diaspora. James's martyrdom (AD 62 or 69) falls within the period that saw Jewish-Roman tensions rising, which led to the First Jewish Revolt (AD 66–70). Violent resistance against Roman governors whose names we read in the New Testament (e.g., Felix and Festus) may very well have been in James's mind as he wrote his circular letter. James might also have been responding to the various theopolitical visions of the Sadducees, Pharisees, and Essenes, each of whom were postured quite differently toward the status quo and believed quite differently about the meaningfulness

33. King, *Stride toward Freedom*, 76.

of human action in the world vis-à-vis fate.[34] We see that James warns against "envy," otherwise translated "zeal." At the very least, violent Zealots might have been for James a cautionary tale from revolts gone by. He might have linked the envy and strife between the haves and the have-nots in the diaspora (cf. James 4:2) to the ongoing political jockeying in the rest of society. Having ministered amid violent forms of disownment, James casts a vision for a peaceable community formed by heavenly wisdom among those who humbly "come near to God" (v. 8). Neglecting social and cultural exegesis of the politically fraught context of James's letter robs modern readers of applying it effectively to our own context.

The biblical prophetic tradition is another important normative resource. The prophetic tradition is realistic about the interventions of the God of justice in history. Additionally, in the New Testament, announcing the inbreaking of God's kingdom and the lordship of Jesus Christ is a prophetic kind of heraldry we now know as evangelism. Dr. King's hopeful sermons and speeches are replete with references to the prophets. After all, the "arc of the moral universe" does not bend effortlessly toward justice as if racial equality were only a matter of time. It does so in the Christian tradition, however, because it is bent by a moral agent—principally, God in the person and work of Jesus Christ—whom we herald and is embodied as a prophetic symbol in God's creation of the family of Christ. To the extent that churches and ministries exercise a prophetic imagination, their ministries extend the prophetic tradition as they engage the social order.

In fact, envisioning and embodying a different social order has been the implicit and explicit business of the church.

34. See Levine, "Visions of Kingdoms," 364.

Even in the era of deeply problematic church growth strategy, highly produced worship services, and professionalized ministries, churches large and small practice diverse and contextual social arrangements—some fashioned more after the dominant culture than others. Be that as it may, critical race theorists would be mistaken to overlook the mobilizing power of religious social consciousness. It bears remembering exemplars like Óscar Romero, Dorothy Day, Martin Luther King Jr., César Chávez, Malcolm X, Allan Boesak, Saint Teresa of Calcutta, William Wilberforce, John Perkins, and others whose spiritual convictions compelled them to engage in practical-prophetic critique even when it was not welcomed within their spiritual communities.

To elaborate on this point, anti-apartheid theologian and clergyman Allan Boesak leverages his Reformed confessional zeal as a tool for social critique within his context. In his rhetoric, he appeals to the liberative aspects of the work of Dutch theologian Abraham Kuyper: "The reformed tradition has a future in this country only if black Reformed Christians are willing to take it up, make it truly their own, and let this tradition once again become what it once was: a champion of the cause of the poor and the oppressed, clinging to the confession of the lordship of Christ and to the supremacy of the word of God."[35] Since many looked to the Kuyperian legacy as a source of the Dutch Reformed Church's racist errors, Boesak's exhortation was a way of renarrating the Dutch Reformed tradition in the face of oppressive Afrikaner nationalism. Boesak and others within the leadership of the Dutch Reformed Mission Church, and later within the World Alliance of Reformed Churches, were energized by the work of reclaiming aspects of their

35. Boesak and Sweetman, *Black and Reformed*, 95.

tradition. They successfully organized an architectonic critique of South African national life by leveraging Kuyper's preferential option for the poor and consciously applying it to the intersection of poverty and racism on behalf of black South Africans. It is truly difficult to conceive of constructive outcomes apart from the kind of persevering engagement that Boesak and many others displayed. This refusal to disown and disavow, while supererogatory, is near the heart of the normative resources of the Christian tradition. I am most inspired when the refusal is not a plaintive whimper but a roaring objection to dispossession. Boesak's renarration was a way of saying, "Mine!" Black Reformed Christians in South Africa would not be dispossessed of their inheritance in the saints.

Presupposing that King's *agapē* could lead to personal, moral transformation is another way of saying, "Mine!" The appeal of separatism grew as the civil rights movement wore on. Eventually, deep skeptics of Kingian theology and ethics proposed that King played respectability politics with white society. It is abundantly obvious that King drew on the political logic of the constitution in order to appeal to the plausibility structures of the watching public. However, when King talked about the constitution as a promissory note in his "I Have a Dream" speech at the Lincoln Memorial, he did not talk about the marchers in the passive voice, as if they were hopelessly dispossessed. Instead, he said, "We've come to cash this check."[36] Against the backdrop of this assertiveness, the discourse of death appears more like capitulation, or even self-dispossession. As far as my experience has informed me, deepening alienation attends those whose discourse is marked by disownment and disavowal.

36. King, "I Have a Dream."

## Revelation 7:9 as Counterstory

John's Revelation will serve as a closing example of eschatological counterstory aimed at pastoring the beloved community. I believe that this is closer to how the text itself functions than, for example, a predictive approach regarding the timing of Jesus's return. Another thin use of the text sees the great multitude from every nation, tribe, people, and language as a symbol of mere representational diversity. Some Christian leaders use this image to fuel their aspirations for racial diversity in their congregations or perhaps for a relational approach to neighborhood evangelism. Approaches to Revelation 7:9 that culminate in a simple call for so-called multiethnicity are in need of both hermeneutical thickness and a more fitting moral analogy.

Regarding hermeneutical nuance, at worst Revelation 7:9 becomes a proof text that provides only token support for efforts to diversify a congregation. Used in this way, the apparent representational diversity in Revelation 7:9 eclipses the rest of the passage, its co-text (i.e., its location and function within the chapter), and its historical context. This would not be as serious a problem if the situation that John describes in the relevant co-texts did not so profoundly impact and shape the imagination behind the words of Revelation 7:9 in the first place. For example, the diverse multitude is worshiping victoriously in white robes, washed in the blood of the Lamb. Brian Blount reflects on this imagery and the African American Christian tradition:

> In their hymns and preaching, African Americans have testified that there is indeed power in the blood of the lamb. That blood, however, does not represent a call to martyrdom; it is an invitation to nonviolent, revolutionary action.

Anthony Pinn argues for "a dissonance between the social body and the black bodies, a discord that sparks and fuels religion as historical liberation because the former operates through a process of bad faith and corrupt intentions." One could argue for the same distance between the social body (expectation of emperor worship) in the witness body or "soul" (which symbolizes resistance to that expectation) in revelation. The spiritual body is in extreme dissonance with the Roman social one. By definition, it is therefore resistant, and actively so. A believer must make an active choice, given the social context of Asia Minor at the end of the first century, to be one type of body or the other. John dramatizes his preference with this horde of souls clothed in robes washed to sparkling sheen in the blood of the lamb. He has essentially reconfigured the dress of execution into the clothing of defiance. All of a sudden, what some might view as a martyr's attire has become the fine, sparkling linen of subversive witness. These dead souls, all dressed up, are a soul force.[37]

Blount takes Roman inducement to worship Caesar with deadly seriousness. John is very tender and affirming of those who have resisted the cult of Caesar, and he is severe with *insiders* who make it more difficult to stand firm in the faith. I recall a conversation with a veteran pastor who insisted that the problem here is temptation to doctrinal error. This pastor refused to see the significance of the pressures of the imperial cult and the allure of economic security by conformity with the economic guilds of the time. To become an inside agent of the imperial cult was to betray the gospel and the people of God. Triumphing over this pressure, John warns through the imagery of 7:9, may involve the spilling

---

37. Blount, *True to Our Native Land*, 536–37. For the quote from Pinn, see *Terror and Triumph*, 96.

of martyr blood, but John's readers can take heart because Jesus's own powerful, sanctifying blood was spilled.

Understood this way, a thicker moral analogy with greater ethical and spiritual significance becomes available to black church communities (and others) that continue to suffer violence. Moral analogies are, according to Richard Hays, "imaginative analogies between the stories told in the texts and the story lived out by our community in a very different historical setting."[38] The analogy is a bridge of sorts, enabling contemporary readers of Scripture to make biblically robust applications. A moral analogy must encompass not only the throne room description but also the situation into which John writes, as well as the "symbolic universe" that John creates for his readers through his use of Old Testament imagery. John's vision transports the reader into the heavenly throne room, where the drama of God's redemption unfolds—sometimes with nearly inexpressible beauty, sometimes with paralyzing horror. Against the immense power of the imperial cult and the insurmountable Roman persecution to come, a symbolic universe is the arena of the triumph of God in the Christian imagination. Unwilling to endanger the churches he loves, John does not name the agents responsible for the churches' persecution. Instead, he uses symbols to tell a story about the triumph of God over the Roman Empire. "The symbolism is meant to stimulate these Christians to see the world as it truly is, not to veil it from their sight until some future generation should discover what twenty centuries of readers had missed all along."[39]

The pastor who prepares a sermon on Revelation 7:9 may be tempted to make a simple comparison between the

38. Hays, *Moral Vision of the New Testament*, 298.
39. Achtemeier, Green, and Thompson, *Introducing the New Testament*, 562. See, for example, John's use of gematria in the number of the beast to gesture at Nero.

diversity language in this passage and multiethnicity in the church. That, however, would say less about the text itself, and it would say next to nothing about the price paid by communities who remain faithful and hopeful for the return of Jesus amid discrimination and persecution.

What this reexamination of Revelation 7:9 makes possible, then, is an understanding of John's imaginative creation of a symbolic universe as a source of community cultural wealth (see the discussion in chap. 1). John's exercise of imagination is an expenditure of a combination of spiritual and resistant capital, two of the components of community cultural wealth. Readers of the book of Revelation who experience marginalization may think that their survival depends on two possible allegiances—to their ecclesial community or to the empire. Such binary thinking is not entirely inaccurate, but it is unnecessarily limiting. Instead, Blount writes regarding the faithful witness, "What must be encouraging at this point is not the realization that more believers will die, but that more believers will fulfill the witness that will transform human history, just as it once transformed cosmic reality. God's justice will come on earth, just as it came in heaven, and their witness will play a vital part."[40] Blount connects this ethical vision to the civil rights movement, which benefited from diverse coalition-building beyond the African American community.

What Christian eschatology contributes to CRT is *not* merely a vision of transformation. CRT already has a sober vision of transformation that spans the breadth of juridical and legislative matters and fires the imagination of activists. Rather, eschatology gives community a particular ethical vision about itself. Anglican priest Michael Battle gets us part

40. Blount, *Can I Get a Witness?*, 64.

of the way there in his theological conclusions about John's Revelation:

> I think John suggests a future direction for humanity in which we stop worrying over dualisms and political deadlock. That we stop conservatism's worry over who is in or out of heaven. That we stop also the liberalism that easily dismisses the value of a nonviolent confessional faith in a world full of violence and conflict. And that we stop the smugness of thinking we have figured out what 666 means or who the dragon is. I hope this book is in concert with John's afterword in which a paradigm shift occurs. The paradigm shift is this—we all scramble in darkness until we see God's reign on earth as it is in heaven.[41]

I appreciate Battle's exemplary evenhandedness and willingness to listen to conservatives and liberals throughout his book. That alone is a model of discourse that is far too rare. I think he's much closer to the purpose of Christian community when he writes, "A strange new church realized that community was not for itself—it was made to glimpse the kingdom of heaven. This mystery of becoming more than who we are has always been God's project of birthing heaven."[42]

The Christian community is not for itself; it is for the blessing of the nations. This is not growth by triumphalist conquest or shrewd evangelism strategy, but somehow, the martyr throng of Revelation 7:9 is part and parcel of what culminates in the nations streaming to the mountain of God to see, hear, and experience shalom. The community grows by resurrection from the dead, by those seeking to lose their

41. Battle, *Heaven on Earth*, 178.
42. Battle, *Heaven on Earth*, 78.

lives for Jesus's sake. Delgado and Stefancic seem uncertain when they write about the value of CRT insight: "Understanding how the dialectic works, and how the scripts and counterscripts work their dismal paralysis may, perhaps, inspire us to continue even though the path is long and the night dark."[43] By contrast, the explosive power of the resurrection creates the space to envision the future victory of God over the principalities and powers in our time, which makes John's Revelation a source of light and warmth.

## Conclusion: Resting and Restless

In two ways, I have found that a thin eschatology creates trouble for the people of God. On the one hand, by placing our trust—even subconsciously or by the false asepsis of omission—in the systems and structures that work well enough for us but that dispossess our neighbor, we conveniently forget the disruptive coming reign and rule of God in Christ. We may say that God's justice is otherworldly and that God's ways are higher than ours, but we live placidly, as though there is little left to be done in the world, choosing instead to focus on private spiritual delights. The restlessness this generates in Christians who hunger and thirst for righteousness is readily observable to anyone who possesses ears to hear and eyes to see.

That restlessness, on the other hand, can lead us to febrile trust in our own agency and our own vision of the future. We may say that God's justice is otherworldly, and that God's ways are higher than ours, but we work as though our own cultural capital, knowledge, and imagination approximate the resources and redemptive plan of the God who brought

---

43. Delgado and Stefancic, "Images of the Outsider," 1291.

Israel out of Egypt by God's own liberating might. The racial trauma and burnout of precious ones who struggle to spy sabbatical shores is skyrocketing.

All that said, who knows whether or how long my family and I will be able to endure the rough seas of our racially fractious moment? We covet the warmth and friendship of our beloved community and the prayers of those who keep their eyes fixed on an eschatological horizon—a promise of entering the real presence of the resurrected Lord of the Sabbath—when we can scarcely lift our heads.

# Conclusion

## Made to Be Image Bearers

We are made to be image bearers. According to God's original plan at creation, as women and men, we were intended to worship God and reflect God's loving stewardship over all of creation (Gen. 1:27). In faithfulness to God's command, we are to "multiply and fill the earth" (Gen. 1:28 ESV) and, as a natural outcome of interacting with God's diverse creation, give birth to the different ethnic groups of the world, each with their distinct cultural treasures and wealth, or "glory and honor" (Rev. 21:26; see also Hag. 2:7). In the language of CRT, we all possess valuable and unique community cultural wealth. A central contention of this book has been that we each uniquely reflect God's glory and image in the world through the cultural treasures that God has given us. On the flip side, as a direct consequence of the fall and humankind's turning away from God, sin entered the world, causing the divine image in each of us to become corrupted. This corruption includes sin's infection of our different cultural treasures (Rev. 21:27). Christ gave his life to redeem us as individuals

167

(John 3:16) and to renew our distinct cultural treasures that are of eternal value to God.

Five hundred years of European and Euro-American colonialism greatly distorted the biblical truth that every ethnic group of the world possesses equal and distinct glory and honor. Colonialism created the concept of race as an official legal, social, and political category in order to control power and privilege for Europeans and their descendants in the lands they conquered. The Spanish first invented race in their American colonies through the development of the social and legal categories of "Spanish," "Indian," "black," "mestizo," "mulatto," and even "chino." The English colonies of the so-called New World followed suit and established their own racial system on the socially constructed legal categories of "white" and "black." Whether in the Spanish or English colonies, the explicit and implicit theological message was the same: "We as 'whites' have a monopoly on God's image and the cultural treasure and wealth of the world. 'Indians,' 'blacks,' 'Asians,' and mixed-race peoples have little to no 'glory and honor' compared to us Europeans and our descendants. Moreover, the former have much cultural sin, while those who are socially categorized as 'white' have little to none. If you really want to follow Jesus, then you have to not only believe in him but also shed your inferior culture and become like us." As a consequence, Jesus was turned into a tribal God made in the preferred image of the colonizers. Thankfully there were those such as Bartolomé de las Casas who, from the very beginning of the colonial project in the Americas, challenged such unbiblical logic. Furthermore, colonial societies were structured to dole out socioeconomic and political privilege to those of the preferred race and to withhold such privileges in differing degrees from all others. In the United States, Jim Crow segregation systematized such racism in every facet of life, including housing, health care, education, employment, voting, media, and even church. De jure segregation and explicit racial discrimination were officially banned through the Civil Rights Act of 1964, the Civil Rights Act of 1968, the Voting Rights Act of 1965, and other federal and state laws, but we still feel many painful consequences to the present day.

Critical race theory emerged as an academic discipline in the 1980s because law schools failed to take account of this invidious racial history and its contemporary repercussions in their curriculum and research. CRT soon spread to other fields, such as education, because of similar intellectual voids throughout the academy. Over the years, I (Robert) have come to one basic conclusion: CRT is *helpful*. CRT has given me and thousands of other people of color the language to describe our racialized experiences. It has also been helpful for my own academic teaching and research and has served as a bridge for Christian witness, theological reflection, and pastoral ministry.

As this book has discussed, CRT has become a political bogeyman for millions of people who do not even know what it is. In the heightened political discourse of the past several years, CRT has become shorthand for any academic analysis of racism in the United States, no matter how empirical or objective. In response to any critique of US race relations—even critique offered in the spirit of concern and desire for national healing—the response of those on the far right has become, in essence, "That's not true. The United States is and always has been exceptional. That's just CRT. You're a Marxist. How can you call yourself a Christian?" At the same time, to be fair, there have been some on the far left who have weaponized CRT in a manner that further sows social tensions without the larger picture of the beloved community in mind. Both are true at the same time, and I, with many others, subscribe to neither extreme.

Knee-jerk reactions to CRT can be likened to the manner in which a dysfunctional family responds to conflict between siblings. One sibling raises a concern to their parents about how they were injured or abused by another sibling. Healthy and mature parents receive such serious accusations with care and with a desire to find out what objectively happened so that they can figure out how they might bring justice—and hopefully reconciliation. Unhealthy parents, however, might seek to minimize or even deny that the harmful act ever occurred. Without the facts in hand, they might favor one child over another for emotional reasons. They might even ignore the problem in order to protect themselves from shame and might blame the victim for presenting ungrounded accusations that have disrupted the so-called family peace. This is a recipe for decades of family dysfunction and estrangement between siblings and parents alike. In its worst forms, such denial can allow for the perpetuation of unchecked abusive behaviors and the destruction of other lives.

This family analogy represents the dysfunctional state of racial and cultural affairs in the United States. Out of concern for our US family, and especially our sisters and brothers in the church, some of us are attempting a loving intervention. We are trying to bring to light the ugly history of racism and its pernicious effects so that forgiveness and healing may occur. Some of our other siblings have been attempting to do so for many years and have already grown weary. In order to protect their own health and well-being, and at the advice of their Christian therapists, they have had to distance themselves from the US church and its dysfunctions and denials. By dint of circumstances and God's calling, some of us are like the younger siblings who continue to raise the issues, not because we are troublemakers but because we love our family and want it to heal. We know that reconciliation or conciliation cannot come without responsibility, repentance, and forgiveness. At the same time, we are realistic enough to know that in broken families there are those who choose to reject responsibility, as well as those who avoid the conflict altogether in order to maintain a false sense of peace. We love the family of God too much to stay silent. We resonate deeply with the prophetic proclamation from the book of Jeremiah:

> They dress the wound of my people
> as though it were not serious.
> "Peace, peace," they say,
> when there is no peace.
>
> Jeremiah 6:14

Cheap grace and reconciliation that glosses over the five hundred years of violence and racism that has killed, segregated, deported, and left hungry—this is not the work of the Spirit. No, the Spirit-led process of naming, resonating, repenting, decolonizing, and healing—this is the work of the gospel.[1]

Yet to many in the US church today, this work is considered "mission drift."[2] They are missing the very work of the Spirit that is happening in their midst, in their churches, denominations, Christian colleges and universities, seminaries, and BIPOC-led ministries and organizations. Though more than two thousand verses of the Bible speak about God's heart of

---

1. Romero, *Brown Church*, 214.
2. The following conclusory remarks are drawn from Robert Chao Romero and Erica Shepler Romero, "When BIPOC Leaders Speak Out," *Missio Alliance*, September 3, 2021, https://www.missioalliance.org/when-bipoc-leaders-speak-out/.

justice for immigrants and the poor, many critics respond with a knee-jerk rejection of any meaningful application of these verses to the history or contemporary workings of the United States. Somehow they believe that our country is immune to social sin. Many are quick to claim that sin profoundly affects us all on a personal level, but for some reason, in the next breath they adamantly reject the notion that sin affects the United States on a social and cultural level. Their dismissal is not biblical but sociological. Their social identities are grounded on the underlying assumption that the United States has only ever been an exceptional Christian nation.

As a consequence, any earnest biblical social critique (no matter how gracious or empirically grounded) creates within them a deeply disturbing sense of cognitive dissonance. In response to such internal dissonance, rather than addressing the issues facilitating the dissonance, they double down to try to make the feeling go away. Instead of considering other perspectives from culturally diverse members of the body of Christ who have different life experiences and journeys with Jesus, they reassure themselves by clinging to sources that confirm their bias. To make themselves feel better, they then sling mud and vitriol and say things like, "You're a Marxist. You're a follower of CRT. You are divisive. God is color-blind. If you don't like the United States, then leave!"

I have observed that it is largely black, Latina/o, Asian American, and Native American sisters and brothers in Christ who have taken the hits in these types of intercultural exchanges. Though church and ministry leaders say they value our diverse perspectives and cultural backgrounds, we are the ones who end up getting punished for the cognitive dissonance that some feel when we simply share our voice. They want the color of our skin in their pews but don't want the different perspectives that flow from our unique experiences of journeying with Jesus in our different color skin.

Our jobs in churches, Christian colleges, seminaries, and nonprofits are the ones getting put on the chopping block of white nationalism in order to pacify disgruntled staff and donors. Our ministries get cut and defunded. We get the bad performance reviews and are passed up for promotion in favor of the token minority- or majority-culture Christian who is less qualified or who never rocks the boat. Did we do anything unbiblical? Quite the contrary. We love Jesus with all our hearts and simply apply sacred Scripture to our life contexts and ministries. And we even bear much fruit for the kingdom! But in doing so, we also make some people feel uncomfortable, and so we pay the price.

To our dear friends and leaders who have been speaking up, have been loving teachers and prophets, and have been helping people sift these toxins from our faith: thank you.

We see you.

To the leadership of predominantly white churches and denominations, Christian colleges and seminaries, parachurch ministries, and nonprofits: We pray that you will listen to the prophetic voices that remain and feel the pain of those who have paid a high cost to speak up. We must not heed the voices of those who have not recognized, spoken against, or repented of the ever-increasing white Christian nationalism in the evangelical church. We do not trust their spiritual discernment—and we should be especially wary of those who call themselves teachers, theologians, and missionaries without having repented of these wrongs or humbled themselves enough to consider the perspectives of others in the body of Christ. As Paul has warned us in the sacred words of Scripture, this is a recipe for division and does not reflect the heart of God (1 Cor. 12:24–26).

We are praying for the soul of the US church, that such toxic leaders would be sifted out and would exhibit a deep repentance—which would be a testimony to the watching world.

We pray for the BIPOC and white leaders who have counted the cost and spoken the truth in love—that they will receive the comfort and strength they need to continue in their God-given prophetic and pastoral callings. Like the prophets of old, you are now being persecuted, but it is through you that the US church will grow "to become in every respect the mature body of him who is the head, that is, Christ" (Eph. 4:15). This is "so that the body of Christ may be built up until we all reach unity in the faith and in the knowledge of the Son of God and become mature, attaining to the whole measure of the fullness of Christ" (Eph. 4:12–13).

It just so happens that as I (Jeff) write these concluding thoughts, I have just returned from two weeks in South Africa, where I and two others from Fuller Seminary spent time learning from South African professors and ministers about race, history, and public theology. I was surprised and encouraged by the way ministries like the Warehouse in Cape Town hold together liberation, community development, and the authority of Scripture, all within the life of the local church. I was even more surprised and encouraged by the way the label *evangelical* and the work of liberation were not worlds apart as they seem to be here in the United States. Only thirty-one years after the repeal of apartheid legislation, the way social life is arranged—including the various churches and Christian movements—demonstrates the intransigence of racial injustice. Alas, if the decades since emancipation and subsequent civil rights victories are not enough time to reform social arrangements in the United States, then we cannot count on time alone.

Years ago, and oceans away, I peered into the theology of apartheid from the racialized society here in the United States. My reading and research generated a hunch about the kinds of theology that are vulnerable to racist and nationalist distortion. In 2019, my denomination, the Christian Reformed Church of North America, declared the theology of kinism—an apartheid-like theology that prescribes racial separation and opposes interracial marriage—heresy. Knowing what I knew about the Dutch Reformed Church in South Africa and its justification of apartheid, I was not surprised to hear about kinists within the ranks of my historically Dutch denomination.

During the civil rights movement, this denomination (like many others) fiercely debated the ethics of ecclesial involvement in the struggle for racial justice. Simplistic and sophisticated theologies that upheld the status quo were offered; theologies that challenged the status quo were also offered. I came away from my reading acquainted with the racialized, theological "common sense" of those who were willing to effectively leave well enough alone. Christian ethics, it turned out, was the province of the individual conscience, not the church *as* church. I have attempted to "call in" those who hold to primarily individualistic culpability thinking. There is more in the Scripture than that. Additionally, the sincere piety and relational goodwill of private individuals simply have not achieved the society-wide "reconciliation" that was promised from so many pulpits. It is *not* that the ethos of the Promise Keepers in the 1980s or the convictions of the Southern Baptist Convention's statement "The Christian and the Social Order" were untried and found wanting. Rather, generations of Christians in the United States have been nourished by this theology and have allowed it to shape their "common sense." Most other unconventional prescriptions *are* left untried and found wanting—including those prescriptions from communities of color that have survived racial discrimination with their love for God and neighbor intact.

What my coauthor, Robert, has found helpful about CRT, I have found deeply forming and comforting. Learning to question and eventually challenge the "common sense" that does not comport with the history, habits, and hermeneutical inclinations that God has granted my people was nerveracking at first. Learning that critical questions about individual liberalism, color blindness, and unjust hierarchies can be found both in CRT *and* throughout so much Christian theology has, at the very least, taught me that it doesn't have to be this way. There are theologies that don't separate material realities from spiritual realities, verbal proclamation from works of righteousness, or common humanity from pluriform particularity.

If social media is an indicator of *any* kind, young people are less and less hesitant to critique, disown, and disavow the "common sense" of previous generations. Typically, it is either the ethical and judicial conclusions or the unpopular characterizations of antiquated convictions that become the butt of jokes or the subject of derision. Studying theology has taught me that it doesn't have to be this way. There are (and have been) theologies—even evangelical theologies—of liberation that defy dismissive stereotyping. What's more important, however, is that there are people of the covenant on whose faithful legacy we stand—a great cloud of witnesses, a beloved community that transcends time and geography. This is part and parcel of the Christianity toward which we are gesturing in this book.

We do so, in part, because we are bound as ministers to the entire covenant people whom Christ—the One who in his baptism bound himself to us—came to love, to die for, to save, to raise to new life, and to make into a new humanity. To keep the "communal" in communion, we remember not only the broken body and shed blood of Jesus but also the unlovely community he calls "beloved." In fact, when I speak the Words of Institution, I sometimes like to pause ever so briefly after the first line in my tradition's recitation: "On the night he was betrayed . . ." Many words follow, but as the bread and the cup pass my lips, my mind wanders back to betrayal.

I have been betrayed.
I have betrayed others.
I have been disowned.
I have disowned others.

If I am bold enough to raise my eyes to the sanctuary cross while I examine myself, there on the eschatological horizon is the fierce and effective love of God in Christ Jesus, which forges bonds where there was once betrayal. My pardon and my liberation are not for me alone but are so that I may worship God with God's people and in God's place and may pursue God's purposes for others to do the same.

I can't write or speak about a communal-covenantal vision of life without skeptics objecting to the dewy-eyed absurdity of it all. In fact, such a central, normative motif of the Christian tradition as loving one's enemies is now considered by a growing number to be a veiled form of social control that oppresses people who suffer abuse. No shepherd who loves their sheep should casually write off the horrors and pains behind this critique.

Robert has addressed leaders and bespoken our prayerful hope for you as leaders. I'd like to conclude by addressing family and friends adrift, longing for welcome.

We see you.

To the quiet exodus of young people who feel unpursued, bearing open and active wounds, and feel raw and enraged by the grievous sins of the churches they once called home: We pray that desert wandering does not last longer than your soul can bear. While you journey through dry lands, we pray that you'll encounter streams in the desert, the surprise of beloved community, and the very person of Jesus by the Holy Spirit, our helper and advocate. We pray that you'll be delivered from violence of spirit (yours and others') in ways we were not, that you'll succeed in ways we have failed. We pray that you will resist the discourse of death with the living Christ's love of neighbor and even of enemy. Finally, we pray that the noisomeness of the culture wars would neither misshape your affections nor drain your energy as you faithfully bear witness to the love of God among your friends and neighbors, for God alone is good.

# Glossary

**capital:** Assets, which can come in many forms, including but not limited to money. We refer to forms of social capital that are constituted by and operate within aspects of human cultures.

**color blindness:** From a legal perspective, an opposition to proactive measures aimed at remedying the effects of racial injustice and the denial of the present existence of structural or systemic racism on a significant scale.

**community cultural wealth:** In the context of urban educational studies, the cultural treasure that students of color bring to their education. This is distinct from, but not inferior to, the social capital of white students. This wealth corresponds to the biblical notion of the "glory and honor of the nations" (Rev. 21:26).

**critical race counterstories:** Narratives involving composite characters drawn from social science data, interviews, and personal experience. These narratives are used to dispel stereotypes and to bring to light the personal and corporate experiences of people of color.

**critical race theory (CRT):** A diverse, multidisciplinary field of study that examines the role of race in the development of US law and policy.

**idealism:** A way of seeing the world in terms of ideas rather than, among other things, human experience.

**interest convergence:** A CRT principle that claims that majority white society rarely supports the passage of civil rights laws and policies for ethnic minorities without an underlying element of self-interest.

**intersectionality:** The observation that humans inhabit more than one social identity and that race, therefore, should not be considered in isolation from gender or other social identities.

**liberalism:** A political philosophy that emphasizes individual liberties, private property, and free enterprise.

**microaggressions:** In the context of race, small acts of racism that are experienced by people of color and that collectively exact a heavy emotional burden.

**"Racism is ordinary":** A basic tenet of CRT that asserts that racism is a normal and regular occurrence within US society, as opposed to something out of the ordinary.

**social construction thesis:** The idea that racial categories are socially constructed rather than biological in nature.

**systems and structures:** Patterns in our social world, including but not limited to interpersonal relationships, that can be observable or invisible and that relate components of society—for example, people and institutions—to one another.

**voice of color thesis:** A basic CRT tenet that asserts that people of color are in the best position to understand and communicate matters of race in light of their own firsthand experience.

**white by law:** The notion that the term *white* was originally a legal category as opposed to a neutral ethnic descriptor. Those assigned to this legal category by the courts were granted privileged socioeconomic status and political benefits and were spared from segregation.

**worldviewism:** A particular commitment to constructing and living a worldview that competes with other worldviews for verity or authenticity.

# Bibliography

Achtemeier, Paul J., Joel B. Green, and Marianne Meye Thompson. *Introducing the New Testament: Its Literature and Theology*. Grand Rapids: Eerdmans, 2001.

Anzaldúa, Gloria. *Borderlands/La Frontera*. San Francisco: Aunt Lute Book Company, 1987.

Baker, Bruce D., Danielle Farrie, and David Sciarra. *Is School Funding Fair? A National Report Card*. 7th ed. Newark, NJ: Education Law Center, 2018. https://edlawcenter.org/assets/files/pdfs/publications/Is_School_Funding_Fair_7th_Editi.pdf.

Battle, Michael. *Heaven on Earth: God's Call to Community in the Book of Revelation*. Louisville: Westminster John Knox, 2017.

Beilby, James, and Paul R. Eddy. *The Nature of the Atonement: Four Views*. Downers Grove, IL: IVP Academic, 2006.

Bell, Derrick. "Racial Realism." *Connecticut Law Review* 24, no. 2 (1992): 363–79.

Blount, Brian K. *Can I Get a Witness? Reading Revelation through African American Culture*. Louisville: Westminster John Knox, 2005.

———, ed. *True to Our Native Land: An African American New Testament Commentary*. Minneapolis: Fortress, 2007.

Boesak, Allan Aubrey, and Leonard Sweetman. *Black and Reformed: Apartheid, Liberation, and the Calvinist Tradition*. Maryknoll, NY: Orbis Books, 1984.

Bonilla-Silva, Eduardo. "More than Prejudice: Restatement, Reflections, and New Directions in Critical Race Theory." *Sociology of Race and Ethnicity* 1, no. 1 (2015): 73–87.

———. "Rethinking Racism: Toward a Structuralist Interpretation." *American Sociological Review* 62, no. 3 (June 1997): 465–80.

Carter, Craig A. *Rethinking Christ and Culture: A Post-Christendom Perspective*. Grand Rapids: Brazos, 2007.

Carter, Warren. "Accommodating 'Jezebel' and Withdrawing John: Negotiating Empire in Revelation Then and Now." *Interpretation* 63, no. 1 (2009): 32–47.

Charles, Mark, and Soong-Chan Rah. *Unsettling Truths: The Ongoing, Dehumanizing Legacy of the Doctrine of Discovery*. Downers Grove, IL: InterVarsity, 2019.

Christian, Johnna, and Shenique S. Thomas. "Examining the Intersections of Race, Gender, and Mass Imprisonment." *Journal of Ethnicity in Criminal Justice* 7, no. 1 (2009): 69–84.

Cole, Mike. *Critical Race Theory and Education: A Marxist Response*. New York: Palgrave MacMillan, 2009.

Conde-Frazier, Elizabeth. *Atando Cabos: Latinx Contributions to Theological Education*. Grand Rapids: Eerdmans, 2021.

Cook, Anthony. "Beyond Critical Legal Studies: The Reconstructive Theology of Dr. Martin Luther King, Jr." *Harvard Law Review* 103, no. 5 (March 1990): 985–1044.

Costas, Orlando. *Christ outside the Gate: Mission beyond Christendom*. Eugene, OR: Wipf & Stock, 2005.

De La Torre, Miguel A., and Edwin David Aponte. *Introducing Latino/a Theologies*. Maryknoll, NY: Orbis Books, 2001.

Delgado, Richard, and Jean Stefancic. *Critical Race Theory: An Introduction*. 3rd ed. New York: New York University Press, 2017.

———. "Images of the Outsider in American Law and Culture: Can Free Expression Remedy Systemic Social Ills." *Cornell Law Review* 77, no. 6 (September 1992): 1258–97.

Du Bois, W. E. B. *The Souls of Black Folk: Essays and Sketches*. Chicago: McClurg, 1903. Reprint, New Haven: Yale University Press, 2015.

Dyrness, William. *Poetic Theology: God and the Poetics of Everyday Life*. Grand Rapids: Eerdmans, 2011.

Elizondo, Virgilio. *Galilean Journey: The Mexican-American Promise.* Maryknoll, NY: Orbis Books, 2005.

Emerson, Michael, and Christian Smith. *Divided by Faith: Evangelical Religion and the Problem of Race in America.* Oxford: Oxford University Press, 2000.

Evans, James H., Jr. *We Have Been Believers: An African American Systematic Theology.* Minneapolis: Fortress, 2012.

Frey, William H. *Diversity Explosion.* Washington, DC: Brookings Institution, 2014.

Fuller, Bruce, Yoonjeon Kim, Claudia Galindo, Shruti Bathia, Margaret Bridges, Greg J. Duncan, and Isabel García Valdivia. "Worsening School Segregation for Latino Children?" *Educational Researcher* 48, no. 7 (2019): 407–20.

Gómez, Laura. *Manifest Destinies: The Making of the Mexican American Race.* New York: New York University Press, 2007.

González, Justo. *For the Healing of the Nations: The Book of Revelation in an Age of Cultural Conflict.* Maryknoll, NY: Orbis Books, 2005.

———. *The History of Theological Education.* Nashville: Abingdon, 2015.

———. *Tres meses en la escuela del espíritu.* Nashville: Abingdon, 1997.

Gorman, Michael J. *Reading Revelation Responsibly: Uncivil Worship and Witness; Following the Lamb into the New Creation.* Eugene, OR: Cascade Books, 2010.

Guinier, Lani, and Gerald Torres. "Changing the Wind: Notes toward a Demosprudence of Law and Social Movements." *Yale Law Journal* 123, no. 8 (June 2014). https://www.yalelawjournal.org/article/changing-the-wind-notes-toward-a-demosprudence-of-law-and-social-movements.

Gunsalus González, Catherine, and Justo Luis González. *Vision at Patmos: A Study of the Book of Revelation.* Eugene, OR: Wipf & Stock, 1978.

Haney López, Ian. "'A Nation of Minorities': Race, Ethnicity, and Reactionary Colorblindness." *Stanford Law Review* 59, no. 4 (2007): 985–1064.

———. *White by Law: The Legal Construction of Race.* New York: New York University Press, 2006.

Harris, Cheryl. "Whiteness as Property." *Harvard Law Review* (1993): 1707–91.

Hays, Richard B. *The Moral Vision of the New Testament: Community, Cross, New Creation; A Contemporary Introduction to New Testament Ethics*. San Francisco: Harper, 1996.

Hicks, Derek S. "Eschatology in African American Theology." In *The Oxford Handbook of African American Theology*, edited by Katie G. Cannon and Anthony B. Pinn, 242–52. New York: Oxford University Press, 2014.

Hill, Johnny Bernard. *Prophetic Rage: A Postcolonial Theology of Liberation*. Grand Rapids: Eerdmans, 2013.

Hing, Bill Ong. *Making and Remaking Asian America through Immigration Policy, 1850–1890*. Stanford, CA: Stanford University Press, 1993.

Hoffman, John. "Idealism." In *The Cambridge Dictionary of Sociology*, edited by Bryan S. Turner, 277–78. Cambridge: Cambridge University Press, 2006.

Howell, Elizabeth A., Natalia N. Egorova, Teresa Janevic, Michael Brodman, Amy Balbierz, Jennifer Zeitlin, and Paul L. Hebert. "Race and Ethnicity, Medical Insurance, and Within-Hospital Severe Maternal Morbidity Disparities." *Obstetrics and Gynecology* 135, no. 2 (February 2020): 285–93. https://www.ncbi.nlm.nih.gov/pmc/articles/PMC7117864/.

Jennings, Willie James. *Acts*. Louisville: Westminster John Knox, 2017.

———. *After Whiteness: An Education in Belonging*. Grand Rapids: Eerdmans, 2020.

Jun, Alexander, Tabatha L. Jones Jolivet, Allison N. Ash, and Christopher S. Collins. *White Jesus: The Architecture of Racism in Religion and Education*. New York: Peter Lang, 2018.

Keener, Craig. *The Gospel of Matthew: A Socio-Rhetorical Commentary*. Grand Rapids: Eerdmans, 2009.

Kidwell, Clara Sue, Homer Noley, and George E. Tinker. *A Native American Theology*. Maryknoll, NY: Orbis Books, 2001.

King, Martin Luther, Jr. "I Have a Dream." In *The Autobiography of Martin Luther King, Jr.*, edited by Clayborne Carson, chap. 20. The Martin Luther King, Jr. Research and Education Institute, Stanford University. Accessed August 4, 2022. https://kinginstitute.stanford.edu/chapter-20-march-washington.

———. "Nonviolence and Racial Justice." *Christian Century*. February 6, 1957.

———. *Stride toward Freedom: The Montgomery Story*. Boston: Beacon, 2010.

Kwok, Pui Lan. *Introducing Asian Feminist Theology*. Sheffield, UK: Sheffield Academic, 2000.

Lee, Sang Hyun. *From a Liminal Place: An Asian American Theology*. Minneapolis: Fortress, 2010.

Levine, Amy-Jill. "Visions of Kingdoms from Pompey to the First Jewish Revolt." In *The Oxford History of the Biblical World*, edited by Michael D. Coogan, 352–87. New York: Oxford, 1999.

Lincoln, C. Eric, and Lawrence H. Mamiya. *The Black Church in the African American Experience*. Durham, NC: Duke University Press, 1990.

Lipsitz, George, *The Possessive Investment in Whiteness: How White People Profit from Identity Politics*. Philadelphia: Temple University Press, 2006.

Longenecker, Bruce. "Rome, Provincial Cities and the Seven Churches of Revelation 2–3." In *The New Testament in Its First Century Setting: Essays on Context and Background in Honour of B. W. Winter on His 65th Birthday*, edited by P. J. Williams, Andrew D. Clarke, Peter M. Head, and David Instone-Brewer, 281–91. Grand Rapids: Eerdmans, 2004.

Longman, Karen A. *Diversity Matters: Race, Ethnicity, and the Future of Christian Higher Education*. Abilene, TX: Abilene Christian University Press, 2017.

Loyd-Paige, Michelle R., and Michelle D. Williams. *Diversity Playbook: Recommendations and Guidance for Christian Organizations*. Abilene, TX: Abilene Christian University Press, 2021.

Luker, Ralph. "Kingdom of God and Beloved Community in the Thought of Martin Luther King, Jr." In *The Role of Ideas in the Civil Rights South*, edited by Ted Ownby, 39–54. Jackson: University of Mississippi, 2002.

Marsh, Charles. *The Beloved Community: How Faith Shapes Social Justice from the Civil Rights Movement to Today*. New York: Basic Books, 2008.

Martell-Otero, Loida, Zaida Maldonado Pérez, and Elizabeth Conde-Frazier. *Latina Evangélicas: A Theological Survey from the Margins*. Eugene, OR: Cascade Books, 2013.

Menjares, Pete C. "Diversity in the CCCU: The Current State and Implications for the Future." In Longman, *Diversity Matters*, 11–30.

Mouw, Richard. *The Challenges of Cultural Discipleship: Essays in the Line of Abraham Kuyper*. Grand Rapids: Eerdmans, 2011.

Naugle, David K. *Worldview: The History of a Concept*. Grand Rapids: Eerdmans, 2002.

Nouwen, Henri. *Peacework: Prayer, Resistance, Community*. Maryknoll, NY: Orbis Books, 2005.

Obenchain, Alice M., William C. Johnson, and Paul A. Dion. "Institutional Types, Organizational Cultures, and Innovation in Christian Colleges and Universities." *Christian Higher Education* 3, no. 1 (2004): 15–39.

Packer, J. I. "What Did the Cross Achieve?" *Tyndale Bulletin* 25 (1974): 3–45.

Pannenberg, Wolfhart. *Systematic Theology*. Vol. 2. Grand Rapids: Eerdmans, 1994.

Paradise, Brandon. "How Critical Race Theory Marginalizes the African American Christian Tradition." *Michigan Journal of Race and Law* 20 (Fall 2014): 117–211.

Pazmiño, Robert W., and Octavio J. Esqueda. *Anointed Teaching: Partnership with the Holy Spirit*. Salem: Publicaciones Kerigma, 2019.

Pérez Huber, Lindsay. "Challenging Racist Nativist Framing: Acknowledging the Community Cultural Wealth of Undocumented Chicana College Students to Reframe the Immigration Debate." *Harvard Educational Review* 79, no. 4 (2009): 704–30.

Pettit, Becky, and Carmen Gutierrez. "Mass Incarceration and Racial Inequality." *American Journal of Economics and Sociology* 77, nos. 3–4 (2018): 1153–82.

Pieris, Aloysius. *An Asian Theology of Liberation*. Maryknoll, NY: Orbis Books, 1988.

Pinn, Anthony B. *Terror and Triumph: The Nature of Black Religion*. The 2002 Edward Cadbury Lectures. Minneapolis: Fortress, 2003.

Plantinga, Cornelius. *Not the Way It's Supposed to Be: A Breviary of Sin*. Grand Rapids: Eerdmans, 1995.

Posner, Richard A. "Legal Formalism, Legal Realism, and the Interpretation of Statutes and the Constitution." *Case Western Law Review* 37, no. 2 (1987): 179–217.

Powell, John A. "Racial Realism or Racial Despair." *Connecticut Law Review* 24 (January 1, 1991): 533–51.

———. *Racing to Justice: Transforming Our Conceptions of Self and Other to Build an Inclusive Society*. Bloomington: Indiana University Press, 2012.

Rahner, Karl. *Foundations of Christian Faith: An Introduction to the Idea of Christianity*. New York: Crossroad, 1982.

Rios, Peter. *Untold Stories: The Latinx Leadership Experience in Higher Education*. Eugene, OR: Wipf & Stock, 2021.

Rivers, Ishwanzya D., Lori D. Patton, Raquel L. Farmer-Hinton, and Joi D. Lewis. "That Wasn't My Reality: Counter-Narratives of Educational Success as East St. Louis' Educators 'Reimagine' *Savage Inequalities*." *Urban Education* 57, no. 3 (2021): 335–64.

Romero, Robert Chao. *Brown Church: Five Centuries of Latina/o Social Justice, Theology, and Identity*. Downers Grove, IL: IVP Academic, 2020.

———. "Migration as Grace." *International Journal of Urban Transformation* 1 (October 2016): 10–35.

Salvatierra, Alexia, and Brandon Wrencher. *Buried Seeds: Learning from the Vibrant Resilience of Marginalized Christian Communities*. Grand Rapids: Baker Academic, 2022.

Shavers, Vickie L., Charles F. Lynch, and Leon F. Burmeister. "Knowledge of the Tuskegee Study and Its Impact on the Willingness to Participate in Medical Research Studies." *Journal of the National Medical Association* 92, no. 12 (December 2000): 563–72.

Solórzano, Daniel, and Tara Yosso. "Critical Race Methodology: Counter-Storytelling as an Analytical Framework for Education Research." *Qualitative Inquiry* 8, no. 1 (2002): 23–44.

Sun, Chloe T. *Attempt Great Things for God: Theological Education in Diaspora*. Grand Rapids: Eerdmans, 2020.

Taylor, Charles. *A Secular Age*. Gifford Lectures. Cambridge, MA: Belknap, 2007.

Thiselton, Anthony C. *Systematic Theology*. Grand Rapids: Eerdmans, 2015.

Thurman, Howard. *Jesus and the Disinherited*. Boston: Beacon, 1976.

Tisby, Jemar. *The Color of Compromise: The Truth about the American Church's Complicity in Racism*. Grand Rapids: Zondervan, 2020.

Tran, Jonathan. *Asian Americans and the Spirit of Racial Capitalism*. Oxford: Oxford University Press, 2022.

Van Opstal, Sandra Maria. *The Next Worship: Glorifying God in a Diverse World*. Downers Grove, IL: InterVarsity, 2015.

Wallis, Jim. *America's Original Sin: Racism, White Privilege, and the Bridge to a New America*. Grand Rapids: Brazos, 2016.

Yamamori, Tetsunao, and C. René Padilla, eds. *The Local Church, Agent of Transformation: An Ecclesiology for Integral Mission*. Buenos Aires: Kairos Ediciones, 2004.

Yong, Amos. *Renewing the Church by the Spirit: Theological Education after Pentecost*. Grand Rapids: Eerdmans, 2020.

Yosso, Tara J. "Whose Culture Has Capital? A Critical Race Theory Discussion of Community Cultural Wealth." *Race Ethnicity and Education* 8, no. 1 (2005): 69–91.

Yosso, Tara J., and Daniel G. Solórzano. "Conceptualizing a Critical Race Theory in Sociology." In *The Blackwell Companion to Social Inequalities*, edited by Mary Romero and Eric Margolis, 117–46. Malden, MA: Blackwell, 2005.

———. "Leaks in the Chicana and Chicano Educational Pipeline." *Latino Policy and Issues Brief* (UCLA Chicano Studies Research Center) 13 (March 2006).

Yuen, Nancy. *Reel Inequality: Hollywood Actors and Racism*. New Brunswick, NJ: Rutgers University Press, 2016.

# Index

ethics, Christian
  in civil rights movement, 158, 162
  CRT and, 148, 162–64
  and doctrinal and theological com-
    mitments, 69n9, 82, 140–41, 148,
    150n23, 175
  individual view of, 175
evangelicalism. *See* white evangelicals
evangelism, 156
Evans, James, Jr., 82
Expatriation Act (1907), 51

familial capital, 32
food insecurity, 57–58
formal equality, 150, 152
formalism, legal, 149–50
"fragility," 84n27, 91n37
Francis (pope), 92
future, the
  Christian eschatology and, 23–24,
    130–31, 162–64, 177
  CRT and, 149–53

Galilean Theological Center (GTC),
  103–6
Galilee, 46–47
Gandhi, Mahatma, 145
"glory and honor of the nations"
  BIPOC stories of, 47
  vs. color blindness, 129
  community cultural wealth as, 15–16,
    36, 42, 43–44
  vs. cultural sin, 31, 44–46, 47, 60–61,
    168
  multicultural nature of, 14–15, 22, 38,
    42–43, 60–61
  vs. ordinary racism, 48–50
  scriptural references to, 14–15, 29,
    35–36, 38, 42–43
Gómez, Laura, 52
González, Justo
  and AETH, 106
  on church, 37, 60
  on false multiculturalism, 40–41
  on Revelation, 36
  on theological education, 107, 108–9
Goshens, 53
guilt, rhetorical use of, 85
Guinier, Lani, 150

*Hamilton* (musical), 47
Haney López, Ian, 48–49, 50–51, 121–22
Hanh, Thich Nhat, 145
Harris, Cheryl, 10
Hays, Richard, 161
health care, 58, 92
Heritage Foundation, 66
Heschel, Abraham Joshua, 145
Hicks, Derek, 140–41
higher education. *See* Christian higher
  education
Hing, Bill Ong, 52
*Hispanic* (term), 2n1
Hispanic Summer Program, 106
Hispanic theological education, 103–8
Hispanic Theological Initiative, 106
hope, eschatological, 23–24, 60, 130–31,
  162–64, 177
Hwang, Roland, 16

idealism, 86
image of God
  CRT and, 22, 109, 148, 167
  vs. racial categories, 13–14, 74–76,
    168
Immigration Act (1924), 52
Immigration and Nationality Act
  (1965), 53
Immigration and Naturalization Service, 52
inaugurated eschatology, 139
incarceration, mass, 59
indigenous cultures, 3n1, 81, 92, 100
inequality, systemic and structural, 27,
  50, 53–58, 87, 89–90, 121. *See
  also* legal and social categories;
  segregation
institutions. *See* Christian institutions
interest convergence, 9–10

James (biblical author), 155–56
Jennings, Willie, 124
Jesus
  atonement views and, 69
  cultural constructions of, 91, 124–25
  Galilean context of, 46–47
  "Matthew 18 protocol" and, 97
  and multicultural kingdom, 38
  parables of, 111
  renewal through, 167–68